Tracks of the Missing

Tracks of the Missing

Carl Merrison & Hakea Hustler

This is a Magabala Book

LEADING PUBLISHER OF ABORIGINAL AND
TORRES STRAIT ISLANDER STORYTELLERS.

CHANGING THE WORLD, ONE STORY AT A TIME.

First published 2022, reprinted 2022 x2, 2023, 2024
Magabala Books Aboriginal Corporation
1 Bagot Street, Broome, Western Australia
Website: www.magabala.com
Email: sales@magabala.com

Magabala Books receives financial assistance from the Commonwealth Government through the Australia Council, its arts advisory body. The State of Western Australia has made an investment in this project through the Department of Local Government, Sport and Cultural Industries. Magabala Books would like to acknowledge the generous support of the Shire of Broome, Western Australia.

Magabala Books is Australia's only independent Aboriginal and Torres Strait Islander publishing house. Magabala Books acknowledges the Traditional Owners of the Country on which we live and work. We recognise the unbroken connection to traditional lands, waters and cultures. Through what we publish, we honour all our Elders, peoples and stories, past, present and future.

Cover Design Jo Hunt
Typeset & Internal Design by Post Pre-press Group
Printed and bound in Australia by Griffin Press

978-1-922613-26-4 (Print)
978-1-922613-27-1 (ePDF)
978-1-922613-28-8 (ePUB)

A catalogue record for this book is available from the National Library of Australia

We acknowledge our Elders as custodians and teachers to a continuous link to culture, language and tradition; without them we would not have the rich connection to stories past and present that we do today. Thank you to our editor, Shel Sweeney from A Worded Life, for your constant support and guidance in our journey with both our books. Thank you to Thomas Worrigal for being a consultant on police protocol and procedure, as well as bush survival skills. We appreciate family members for being our cultural consultants and early readers. To Spencer from Warmun, we hope you enjoy your name in the story. Dedicated to our grandparents and our fathers who love/d the bush. While this story does have references to some real-life details, this is purely a work of fiction.

CONTENTS

1

ALARM

I walk to school, sweat already dripping down my forehead in the hot morning sun. There is something different about the small town that I can't place. It would be easy to blame it all on the build-up to the wet season ... but there is a suspense in the air ... like lightning about to strike. I walk through the school gates, I see parents huddled in tight groups under the shade of the buildings, their children whispering amongst themselves instead of running around the playground as usual.

'Hey Dek! Did you hear?' Brad asks, waving me over, even hushed his voice sounding way too loud in the tense atmosphere.

'What's happening?' my voice automatically drops to a nervous whisper as I join my mates. I'm on edge, an uneasy feeling churning in my stomach.

'They found old mate from out la station dead,' Spencer butts in, taking over the story. Brad raises his eyebrows frustrated that Spencer has taken the spotlight again. 'You know the one that's always sly grogging our communities?'

'No way?' I reply quietly. Not that an old man dying is worth all the tension around here. There are a million ways someone could die out on the stations: snakebite, horseriding accident, old mine-shafts, stuck without water. Although this old man did make it a bit more interesting. My eyes flick to Michael who is listening on quietly. 'Heart attack or what?'

'Nah, drowned. The cops were all set to leave it but then the old folk made them look again,' Spencer replies, looking around to see if anyone else is listening in. He clearly likes being the one in the group with all the latest information about the situation. 'Might be murder!'

'Well, that's something different in this boring town,' Brad comments. 'Might be an interesting week after all!'

'Aunty Shellene saw him in town the other day stocking up on grog again. Them bottleshop people never ask what one whitefella station worker been grabbing all that alcohol for. Guess they think he keeping it out there for his workers or something. They never make him stick to those grog rules,' Michael drops his voice. 'You'd think one of them cops would have guessed he was selling it on the black market since all us mob knew.'

'Those police come and go from town. Guess they wouldn't suspect an old guy who they have beers with at the tav,' Willum reflects, shrugging his shoulders, 'for that or anything else!'

'Yeah well most of them local police were out there early this morning. You guys know Dad drives trucks, hey? Well he left for a trip at sparrow fart and I heard him talking to Mum on the phone when I woke up,' Spencer continues the story. 'Dad called his station friend when he saw the cops heading out there. His mate said they found old Mr Henry face down in the dam last night and just wrote it off as an accident. Case closed and all that. Until the old people pushed them to look again this morning. Black magic, murder, something suspicious, I don't know. Dad told Mum all the local cops were out that way canvassing the station and interviewing every house on the way into town this morning.'

Parents who usually drop their kids off are milling around and checking their phones. It reminds me of the build-up to the rain, waiting for something to burst.

'If it wasn't an accident ... who do you think did it?' Brad asks, bending closer as if to protect the deep dark secrets we were all about to reveal.

'You'd think there'd be a line of people with something against that old prick,' Michael spits. He should know. Michael couldn't let his grudge go since his brother passed. Guess he didn't need to hold that grudge any more. For a split second I wonder where he was last night.

'Mr Archer!' the principal yells across the yard, motioning to me to come inside. The boys look at me, scoffing with smirks on their faces. Perfect timing.

'Here we go again,' Willum forces a laugh. 'What've you done this time, bra?'

I look around as I shove Willum. No other Mr Archers here. She can't mean me. We have all been called into a principal's office before – but I'm not in town enough to get into any big trouble here! And not at the start of a day when there might have been a murder in town.

I push my hands deep into my pockets. The principal holds open the door, waiting for me as I cross the yard. All eyes turn to me.

'Pretty strange to get called into the principal's office on a day like today,' whispers one girl as I pass. 'He has to be involved.'

'He's one of those out-of-town community boys,' added her friend from behind her hand. 'Who knows what they are capable of?'

'Bet you he murdered the old guy!' declares the other junior dramatically.

This place has gone crazy, I think to myself. How did we go from being a normal school day to hearing gossip about a murder, to me being accused of it by year 7s the next?

I flick the girls a big toothy smile and lick my lips. They gasp, take small steps backwards, and I laugh. As tight as my stomach feels with tension ... it was too easy to get a rise out of those little gossipers. I straighten my mouth and walk up the steps; the principal looks pale as her eyes dart past me scanning the playground nervously. I walk past her into the dark school hallway and hear the office staff arguing.

'It's not my responsibility,' I hear the secretary complaining from the staff room as we pass. 'It's a teacher's job to make sure it's all charged before they leave for excursion. I'm not having this pinned ...'

Their voices are drowned out as I enter through the principal's pale blue office door.

'Come in and sit down,' she says. Her voice is tight and crisp like a crow's, mouth drawn in a hard line. I haven't done anything wrong that I can think of, well not too bad, not lately and not at school. The chair is hard and forces me to sit up straight. I notice a police officer has taken the principal's seat behind the desk, forcing Ms Wilson to perch nervously on a chair next to him.

'This is Officer Thomas. He just has some questions for you about all the recent events,' the principal prattles, as if trying to make the whole conversation happen quicker. I look at her eyebrows raised. What does this new city cop want with me?

'Yeah miss,' I reply. My mouth is dry but my hands are wet. I'm nervous, cautious and a little curious that this might lead to some firsthand insider info.

'It's been a busy morning, that's for sure. We are just trying to sort through all events that might give us a clue about where else to search,' Officer Thomas explains in a rough, low-pitched voice. 'We need to ask you some questions.'

‘What? Why you asking me?’ I laugh a weak nervous laugh. A sick knot begins to tighten in my belly; something is not right.

‘We’ve just had some concerning news, Dek. Mr Henry’s death is chewing up our police resources and now the year twelves are late to return from camp. With the potential of someone dangerous being on the loose, we just want to get to the bottom of it all quickly. We are trying every avenue,’ Ms Wilson’s voice cracks as she quickly rushes into an explanation.

My mind swirls. While it’s common to get caught up in the outback, today is already anything but normal. I quickly scan back through the past week trying to think of anything I can remember about the camp. My heart sinks as I realise it is the camp that my cousin, Brooklyn, is on ... and Jenny.

‘We just need as much information as we can as quickly as we can to find that bus,’ Ms Wilson prattles on.

They are probably just broken down on the side of the road in that old coaster school bus. My mind slowly connects the dots, and I swallow, shocked with the sudden memory. It can’t be. The bus. It was such a silly thing that I’d forgotten about it ... till now. Me and the boys had been kicking the footy around the streets after training when we noticed the school gate was unlocked. We weren't looking for trouble; we were just wandering kind of aimlessly and saw the tantalising option of a place we weren't meant to go. It wasn't the first time we'd hooned around school on the gardener's wheelbarrow, kicked the footy into the basketball hoops, or written our names on the school shed. It had felt good to be in control of the school for brief moments; no one telling us what to do, or how to behave, or who to be or what to become. In those times, we owned the school and pretended that we owned our destinies. No stereotypes, no predetermined roles for us to fill just as society had decided.

That night, which feels like a lifetime ago now, someone had left their tools and scrap metal out from some metalwork project. We'd been using them as ninja stars throwing them at the wooden wall. It had felt powerful throwing them and hearing the thud when they struck where you had aimed. It reminded me of going out bush hunting with spears like our ancestors had. In control, focused, powerful. I'd got a bit cocky and aimed for a tight spot between two support beams on the shed wall. The metal piece had ricocheted into the side of one of the school bus tyres. I'd had a laugh thinking about the principal changing a tyre. I had wondered if they even could. We'd been helping change busted tyres before I even learnt to tie my shoelaces. In that moment I felt bitterness at some of the outsider teachers that think they know it all but don't even bother learning our culture, or the ones that think I'm too dumb to be anything, or the ones that I learn to trust and then they just up and leave. I'd hoped one of them would be the next to drive the bus to take the teachers to some meeting or for an excursion to the nearby waterhole or something. It hadn't even crossed my mind again until now: why would it? I'd been so focused on the football trials I hadn't really made time for much else. I mean the boys and I had done some graffiti on some signs on our way home a week or two ago. Low level, incidental mischief in between hardcore training. Grandfather had me on a curfew for most of our time in town this time too. Reckoned if I was going to give it a proper shot I should rest up and eat right as well as all the training.

I hadn't realised the bus was headed off to school camp. Even if I had, I would never have thought the tyre would hold until they were in the middle of the bush. Surely, it hadn't?

I cannot believe all this mess might be because of *me.*

Should I tell the Officer? Should I admit we'd been killing time before we went home for dinner? Then the thought hits me ... maybe I killed the year 12s!

My mind spins. My palms sweat. I feel sick.

How will the policeman respond?

I keep my mouth shut.

'Is this an interrogation? Aren't I meant to have an adult here or something?' Suddenly defensive. I know too well what can happen in situations like this. Too many things have been pinned on us mob in the past for no good reason. My grandfather always has something to say when the TV flashes with the latest death in custody or racial profiling issue. For a bushman he is smart about politics and city life. Guess he had to be, growing up through all he did. The worst part now, I might be responsible. Blood could be on my hands.

'We are calling all the parents in for a meeting as we speak. Just working our way through names alphabetically, Mr Archer,' the Officer brushes aside my concern.

'The problem is that we are in a race against time, if anything has happened to those students; it could have already been three nights,' Ms Wilson interrupts the Officer before I can say anything. Her voice wobbles, sounding genuinely concerned. 'We will be asking everyone the same questions.'

'We are chasing every lead but we need to find out everything we can quickly. The first forty-eight hours in a case like this really matter. Let's just say we need to hear anything you can tell us,' Officer Thomas explains gruffly, frustration lines forming across his brow.

'We can't get them on the UHF or satellite phone, we made the students leave behind their devices,' Principal Wilson's brow crunches up in worry too. I'm happy she is waffling; it's giving me a moment to try to process all I have remembered. 'I've called ahead to the ranger at the national park who will be checking the camp site and we have one of Officer Thomas's colleagues, which he can hardly spare in the circumstances, scouting out the road. The fact we can't get in touch with them at a time like this means we need to take this very seriously. You remember what happened to the tourists last summer.'

I do. Even though a lot of the country is flat and scrubby, there are large areas of hills, thick trees. The wide open spaces millions of acres across. The missing tourists had taken a side track looking for gold or a waterhole or something and became stranded out bush. The handful of local coppers had recruited some station owners to use their mustering helicopters to do some aerial searches but they reckon it was a needle in a haystack when the outback is so large. One pilot said he could have almost been on top of them and still missed them if their car was covered in red dust or under some of the trees.

If their tyre did puncture out there ... it could be a long time before the missing students are found. Worse, if a murderer is involved, there are lots of places to hide bodies. It still felt like a bit of a tenuous link that Officer Thomas was trying to make though – a suspected murder linked in any way to the school camp. My mistake is more likely, and that makes my blood run cold.

'Well, I don't know anything about the camp,' I reply, my head spinning trying to think through all the scenarios a bus load of students could encounter out bush. The potentially serious nature of it all sinking in. I'm not exactly lying; I didn't know anything about the camp. 'And I certainly don't know about any dead guy!'

'It might be nothing,' Ms Wilson says to herself as much as me. She's showing how out of depth she really is. Ms Wilson is an outback rookie recruited up here from the city to run the school this year. My mates reckon she hasn't really figured it all out about how things work out here. Schools up here often get young staff or new principals. Sometimes I wonder if we are like a little experiment or test before they get their 'real' city jobs.

'Right now, though, we need answers. Do you remember anything strange from this past week?' the Officer butts in over Ms Wilson.

'Nothing at all,' I reply, quickly jiggling my feet, eager to be out of here. Again I'm not lying ... but I am leaving something out. I need to be out of here to think straight, to make a plan. 'The boys and I have been busy training for the state try-outs coming up. It's all I've been thinking about.'

'What are you so anxious about then?' Officer Thomas growls, looking pointedly at my feet. 'I think you know more than you're letting on.'

'I really don't know anything. What could I know?' This isn't turning out like I had thought it would. I care about Brook. And Jenny, more than I should. I'm stressed as hell trying to figure out what I might have done ... and trying to think about what I need to do now. And this policeman isn't letting up.

I need to change the topic and yet squeeze out as much as I can from this copper. I need a head start so I can figure out what to do next. My mind swirls. I can't make the connections properly. 'Why don't you tell me what happened, and I'll tell you if I know anything extra?'

'Well, we have a death in suspicious circumstances and potentially a murderer running about. The year twelves late to arrive. We know they departed school for the bush early Monday morning. Thick bushland. No reception. A Science and Geography camp looking for artefacts and rock samples. I know that no one has seen or heard from them since they left,' Ms Wilson quickly states the facts, eyes averted, wringing her hands in her lap.

'And we know you and your mates are known to cause a bit of trouble around town ... and out on the stations,' the policeman snarls, reminding me of a dingo waiting to pounce. He is obviously unhappy with Ms Wilson's blabbing on about his case.

My body stiffens and I swallow, throat tight. Are they actually trying to link me to this? I'm no angel. I might have messed up with the bus. The year 12s might be in huge trouble right now and I'm stuck in here being accused of what? Murder? Anyone could have been out that way. Everyone has scored sly grog off the old coot. When I was younger stuck in town one time, we had used our quad bikes to go out bush hunting and exploring. We'd ended up further than we had meant to go, out past the stations west of town. It was a proper hot day so we went swimming in some of the waterholes on the property. We hadn't brought water with us and the dam was all murky from the cattle so we ducked into the station homestead to ask for fresh water. Nobody had been home so we just walked up to get a drink from the tap. Of course, old Mr Henry had found us there; he thought we were 'bloody thieving blakfellas' and chased us off his property with his shotgun. I hadn't seen him from that day until the day of Michael's brother's death. I knew the rumours that Mr Henry had gotten himself tied up in something darker were true. Not worth explaining any of that to this mob though. I'd been in a bit of trouble around town before and they wouldn't believe me anyway.

'I literally just found out about old Henry and the bus, Officer,' I say respectfully, more in control than I feel, purposely trying to control my nervous energy. Trying to put on a tough face. 'Sounds like you know a lot more than me.'

I am glad to have some of the facts of it all. I'm going to need them if I want to help the 12s. If I want to find them. If I want to make up for the mother of all mistakes. This is crazy. Nothing too dramatic ever happens in this town: the occasional stolen vehicle, a car rollover, street fight or family feud. People who move up here to work seem to think even that is hectic enough but it's kind of like background noise to us mob here.

After Michael's brother's death I had been really low. I couldn't see any way out. I had a plan how to end it. It was lucky I suppose that Grandfather had noticed and dragged me down to the clinic for a yarn with the psych there. He'd said us mob deal with trauma all the time without even realising that's not what life is like in other places. That stuff isn't just normal background noise to other people. With all that and Michael's brother's death, he said it was okay for it to hurt. In our culture we can't say his name and even people who share his name change it out of respect. That psych knew strategies and stuff that kind of helped. But I don't think he really knew what it was like for me. He hadn't lost people like us community people had. It's hard to understand the death out here if you are just looking at the statistics of road accidents or suicide stats. Even yarning with us mob. That psych hadn't literally dug the graves of loved ones like we have.

If any of those mob on the bus were hurt because of me though, I don't think there would be any way but down for me. I need to be out of here. I need to be helping with the search.

'Really now? No secrets?' Officer Thomas touches his handcuffs, interrupting my train of thought. 'If we find out you've been holding something back ...'

I imagine those handcuffs snapped tightly around my wrists, pinching my skin. My tongue feels like sandpaper in my mouth as I watch him unclip the cuffs from his belt.

2
NOT A USUAL DAY

'We'll be talking to everyone,' Ms Wilson notices my discomfort as I imagine having to wait to find out the fate of the 12s from inside a prison cell. The guilt overwhelming me with nothing I can do to help. It's not really an unlikely scenario. The police have been known to put kids in the cells – like when Dillon mob were caught doing graffiti late one night and the police couldn't find someone to pass them over to, or when Caleb and I got put in the cell to let us sweat it out a bit after being caught out late one night before the cops gave us the hard word. I remember travelling in the back of that tiny, stifling police van wondering if this is where any blakfellas had died in custody, was I sitting where someone had died? I can only imagine that's what this Officer has planned for me if he wants a scapegoat. Ms Wilson touches my shoulder. The light pressure calms me. It reminds me to breathe. I watch with relief as the Officer places the handcuffs with a thud on the table and adjusts himself in the seat to find his pad and paper.

'Tell us what you remember about the last few weeks, then,' the Officer continues to drill, unfolding his notepad and scribbling something illegible on the paper. My mind is everywhere. I'm still trying to process the news let alone think back a week.

'Nothing unusual,' I mumble, finding it hard to make the words come out of my dry mouth. I don't want to give too much away. If I get detained now there is no way I can get out there and make up for what I have done. 'I only got in maybe two weeks ago. I'm usually from out community but come schooling here with my family sometimes.'

'Speak up, son!' Officer Thomas commands. I cringe at his hostile tone.

'What do you want me to say?' I reply. Sitting up taller, I find the courage to stand up for myself. 'I've already explained that I don't know anything about

Mr Henry. I think I need my grandfather here if you want to ask me any more questions.'

Officer Thomas holds his pen still and looks me up and down. I feel like he is looking right through my skin into my bones. Examining my every motive, finding my every secret. I want to wriggle in discomfort but I force myself to sit still and match his glare.

'Okay. Don't leave town. We might need to speak to you again,' he says, pointing me to the door.

Don't leave town? What does he think I am? The murderer? Some kind of deadly sidekick? Human trafficker? International bus hijacker? I am fifteen. Okay, so I may have totally messed up and caused a bus accident. But surely that teacher did a safety check before taking the bus out? Or surely that tyre busted as she reversed out, she would have changed it and they were on their way? Surely. Maybe the damage wasn't even bad at all and those tyres have held up and it is nothing to do with them. The thought of anything happening to Brooklyn or Jenny sends an uneasy shiver down my spine.

I realise that my hands are held in tight balls that feel light and relaxed as I lift them to open the door. At least out here I can make a difference. As

I leave I hear Officer Thomas say something about arranging the volunteer firefighters to do a sweep of the roadsides all the way to the national park. I walk past five other students and their parents waiting on hard plastic chairs and down the school hall. In the staff room someone is sobbing hysterically. They must have called in some of the families specifically to break the news about the bus. I try to sneak a look to see if Brooklyn's mum, my Aunty June, is in there too. I can't see much before the receptionist notices and shuts the door abruptly in my face.

Walking through the schoolyard I notice parents conversing in hushed whispers, eyes flicking at the parents in the different circles, suspicious. A few are crying. I can't see my grandfather or family.

I stand, eyes squinting at the sparse clouds, trying to think. Trying to process what I have just heard. What I have just remembered. Surely that bloody metal didn't have anything to do with them being late back? I know for certain I didn't have anything to do with Old Henry, stupid old fool. It still doesn't make the growing ball in my stomach go away.

I pull out my phone and dial my grandfather. If I could just yarn with him he would know what to do. It goes straight to voicemail. I know some of them were heading out hunting turkey early this morning. I try my Aunty June.

'What na?' she answers, voice tight with worry. 'Where's this bus? It's taking long time. Making a woman worried.'

My throat gets tight. The words of my confession won't crack past my dry lips.

'Don't know, Aunty,' I soften my voice in reply, trying to break any news I have gently. Just not the news that I might have been involved. 'They've got a policeman and ranger looking and they've called in the volunteer firefighter mob. They're not that worried, only cause old man Henry died.'

I cling to my own words of reassurance. Any other day a late bus wouldn't be big news. I'm sure they are okay. They have to be.

'Well, that old fool's dead now but they better bring my girl home safe. Bloody school!' she mutters, frustrated on the other end of the line.

'They tried calling me in too. I'm better off here with your uncles trying to figure out what to do about it all now,' Aunty June calms her breathing and tells me the plan. 'We aren't worried about our lot being safe out bush. You kids grew up running around bare-foot and snotty-nosed in the red dirt. It's just some of the Elders are really touchy about old Henry's death. They think something else is at work here.'

'Yeah I agree Aunty,' I reply. The thought that it could be something else is something to cling my hope to at least. 'They heading out now or what?'

'I'll let you know kiddo,' she replies. 'Get back to class until we know more.'

I hate when she calls me kiddo and any other time I might bite back. Might argue that I'm coming home now to help out. Not today, she's got enough to worry about.

I don't want to go to class. I want to find my grandfather. I want to get out bush. And as much as I want to help with the search, I want to sink in a corner and disappear into the ground. I'm torn and confused and overwhelmed with the immense weight of the possibilities. How did it come to this? Struck by indecision, my feet automatically walk me towards my class.

I walk into class, late. All eyes turn to me. Not a lot of eyes though; I notice through my fog that half our class is absent today.

'Enough, look this way!' our English teacher demands. 'I know we are all worried about this business out on the station and the year twelves, but we can't do anything about that. We have a test coming up next week, let's just focus on what we can work on. What do you think the author intended with this paragraph ... Marcus?'

I slip in next to Willum and slouch in my chair. I pull out my workbook and pretend to write whatever it is the teacher is still talking about. I can't focus. Willum raises his eyebrows.

'What na?' he mouths. 'What's that all about?'

'It was intense. They seem to think it's more than just a delay. They are checking if Henry's death was more than just an accident ... and if it's any danger to the year twelves,' I don't share the growing lumpy knot of dread that is sitting in my belly. I want to remind him about the mucking around we had done with the bus but I can't figure it all out myself yet and the teacher is shooting us one of those 'quiet or else' teacher death stares.

I wait for the teacher's gaze to move on. 'Where is everyone?'

'Reckon those other parents kept them home when they heard the news,' he replies, flicking his eyes around the classroom himself.

Just as Willum finishes his sentence, there is a knock at the door.

'Sandy?' the school receptionist pops her head around the doorframe. 'Your parents are here to pick you up.'

'See,' Willum whispers as Sandy packs up her books and stuffs them into her bag. 'Lots of them mob will be picking their kids up when they find out too! Rumours spread quickly around here, you know that. Afraid of mass murderers I suppose!'

By 'them mob' he means the kids from the other end of town. My Aunty June lives down the bottom end of town; those other kids live at 'Top area'. We call them the 'high-class' kids. It's kind of strange that the divide is still here from the old days when the blakfella lived in missions on the outskirts of town. The rent down my aunt's end of town is cheaper and has workers' accommodation, so when I was in town, I grew up hanging out with the poorer or middle-class white families too.

Officer Thomas isn't messing around. In quick succession, alphabetically, everyone else is getting called up to the principal's office to recall anything strange they may have seen in the past few weeks. Between interruptions I whisper to my mates to find out more. I leave out my gut-wrenching dilemma. I still need time to figure it out myself. My mates are asked if they knew who the teenagers seen out at the station a few nights before were, if they saw anyone suspicious hanging around the schoolyard or just out of town, if they heard any of the year 12s themselves planning any pranks, if they knew if Mr Henry had any enemies, and where they were on the night before all year 12s fell out of phone reception. From what I knew, the mob out in the communities put up with Henry being sleazy and his bad sense of humour cause he brought the grog out for parties and weekends. The Elders tolerated him cause he'd lived out here for a long time and was boss to a few of our mob. People had started to get a bit edgier with him since rumours started that he was dealing harder stuff to community mob. I knew they weren't rumours. I wish they were.

I'd been hanging out with Michael's brother and his mate Dean on the weekend in town a few months back. The boys had been selling weed low key in town for a while. When they were cashed up they didn't mind me tagging along scabbing chips from the roadhouse with them. That night though, they got word that their supplier had a new shipment in. Dean had tried to dump me at my aunt's but I'd sworn I wouldn't get in their way. My mouth had nearly dropped to the floor when we'd pulled up at the mechanic yard to see old Henry and Clayton's dad. I'd hung around by the gate keeping watch. I'd felt sick when my mates came walking back with the white powder instead of the usual gunja. I'm no angel but that stuff's gross. One thing our mob getting drunk or stoned. I knew that stuff gets you proper hooked. I'd made some excuse then to head back home. I'd left them. And it still hurts.

I wonder if any of that had come out in Officer Thomas's interviews. Then again I know it didn't. Not even Michael knew I was there the night his brother died.

I can't take it any more. I didn't do enough that night. I'll be blowed if I sit around this time. We have to do something to help.

Wait a few minutes then ask if you can go to the toilet, drink or sickbay or that your mum text saying to get picked up at the office or something. Meet me at the back of the library.

I pass the notes around to my mates and they nod in acknowledgement. You wouldn't get away with so many of us getting out of class on a normal day. Mr Rubens is usually pretty tough but I can tell he is a bit flustered with all the interruptions. He has already let a group of girls go to the toilet for ages. I wait for them to come back and make a T toilet sign with my hands. Mr Rubens is mid instructions and waves me out. He doesn't notice that I grab my bag on the way out too.

3

TECH DETECTIVES

The library is the only place where teachers won't ask us why we are out of class. The librarian hardly looks up from her office desk as I walk in. I walk down the back corner to the tables behind some high bookshelves. Willum, Brad and James join me. We all know we wouldn't even have a chance getting Spencer and Michael out of Ms Matthews class; we'll have to fill them in later.

'That was quick,' I say in greeting.

'Don't think Mr Rubens even knows who is meant to be in class or not today,' Willum replies, smile flickering on his lips.

'This is intense,' Brad says. 'What do you guys think?'

'It's gonna just be the fellas playing a trick,' James replies. 'They will have just been mucking around and got delayed.'

'You fellas remember that arvo when we were mucking around at school?' I start slowly, trying to think of the words, wishing one of them would interrupt me and tell me I was wrong. 'I think I might have damaged the tyres of that bus.'

'Nah, bro,' James says quickly, 'impossible that those tyres were still even pumped by the time they left for that camp.'

'If they had a crash or something because of you,' Willum growls, his hands balled into fists, 'I'd make you pain just as bad as they did.'

James quickly steps in between us, moving us behind the shelves out of the librarian's view.

'Unlikely,' Brad soothes, agreeing with James, 'that Dek had anything to do with it. Probably just Ms Pritchard forgot to top up with petrol or something!'

Willum's eyes burn with smouldering anger and deep worry; he pushes James's hands off him. I'm kind of relieved the fellas brushed off our involvement so easily. But that doesn't still the growing sense of fear building in my belly.

‘Aunty June said some of our uncles are trying to figure out what to do next,’ I say slowly, processing what this might mean for me and the boys. Grandfather and I had come back into town from our community a few hundred kilometres out so I could play in the football carnival that was happening tonight. It was a big opportunity: state recruiters for the under 16s team were coming to watch the match. I’m so bloody torn. I need to help.

‘Good, but those mob could take all day talking with family and deciding,’ Willum replies quickly, shuffling back and forth on his feet, his anxiety making him move. ‘We need to get out there.’

‘If anything has happened to Brooklyn I’ll never forgive myself for sitting around school doing nothing,’ I say, leaving Jenny, my forbidden secret, out of it. I hadn’t paid attention to who else was on the camp; my mind had been too preoccupied with the game.

‘One family member stuck out there with a bunch of town kids is bad enough isn’t it? She is family, Dek,’ Willum insists. ‘Even if we didn’t mess up the bus, we can’t just leave her out there when there might be a murderer on the loose? With some posh city teacher who would get lost on a straight highway. They might have crashed and be lying dying? You don’t know.’

'I don't know, that's just it!' I bite back. My mind running in overdrive thinking through all the possibilities. I know we are probably just overreacting, but the tight ball in my belly continues to grow. Something doesn't feel right. Like a word trying to push its way to the tip of my tongue. I try to push it back down. The boys were right, we couldn't have anything to do with the bus running late. They'll be fine and rock up soon, everyone laughing at all the drama. Maybe I should just stay and do the footy trial. I've got to prove to my dad and mates back home that I'm not just a loser. That maybe I can make something of this once in a lifetime chance. But if anything happened to the girls I'd be a loser for waiting around.

I try to remember who I'd seen at school this past week. I don't know a lot of the mob at this school. The kids of teachers, doctors, social workers all come and go every year. I knew most of the locals or at least their families from my stints in town.

I'd noticed some faces from my classes watching on the sidelines of the oval as we trained but that's about it. Had Miranda been running around the netball courts with her friends? Had Clayton and his group been smoking behind the sports shed? Hannah sneering or pointing if anyone missed a shot at goal, daring anyone to call her out on it, thinking she was untouchable? I didn't know all the faces of the kids here though – this school is a lot bigger than our little community school back home. Still the kids who went schooling away said that city boarding schools are way bigger.

'If it helps I think most of the class went. I think it was an assessment or something,' James says. The whole class of year 12 is less than fifteen students, Jenny included. She is smart and a deadly sports player. Her family comes from out my way too. The boys don't know how I feel about her. Or at least not properly. Jenny is the wrong skin for me. She is forbidden.

'We know Brooklyn was on the bus,' Willum adds, concern fleeting across his features. 'And Aaron.'

My family is related to Michael and Brooklyn's mob through our great-grandparents. Their families moved away from our community looking for work in the early days when equal pay came in and lots of station owners kicked us mob off their stations. Brooklyn has beautiful dark skin and long curly hair which she hates. I think she looks like our great-grandmother in the old black-and-white photographs: beautiful and powerful. When their family would visit, we used to run around out in the bush together when we were little. We always stay with them when we come into town. I know she's tough, but that doesn't stop my stomach knotting at the thought of her hurt in a bus somewhere.

As my mates rattle off the names of the students my mind wanders to all the missing year 12s that I know. Dixon is a deadly rugby player; he might even make the state team if he decides to school away at boarding school in the city. Aaron and Willum hang out sometimes when Aaron isn't with his older mates. Miranda is one of the most popular girls in this school, deadly at basketball, quick sense of humour and wicked fashion sense. Clayton's dad is a truckie, I think that's where he picked up his foul mouth. He's the one that supplied Dean and Michael's brother that night. Hannah and all her stubbornness.

'So ... should we just head back to my place to wait for news?' Brad asks, assuming we are just escaping class.

'Nah, we have to do something,' I reply. 'I can't just sit and wait knowing they are out there.'

'What can we possibly do that the cops haven't already started to do?' James scoffs.

'A handful of cops, millions of acres? I don't know but some of us mob grew up out bush most of the time. I need to be there,' Willum replies. 'I'm gonna grab one of them dirt bikes and ride out.'

'Sit down, Willum, you goose,' James scoffs. 'You boys haven't even thought this through properly!'

'What's there to think through, James? That's our family out there. Us mob don't give up on each other like you lot do,' Willum growls back. Family came first with us. In a deeper way maybe than in James's culture. We had complex, deep ties and cultural responsibilities he still didn't understand. 'Plus our uncles have probably already started to organise a search party. We can't miss out on finding out what our mob have planned.'

'Hey!' Brad interrupts. 'This isn't about white and black! When did we ever talk rubbish like that? We are all on the same side. We all want them back.'

'Yeah but these two are forgetting we have the match tonight. They can't just go walkabout looking for the year twelves,' James replies quietly, hurt by the sharpness of Willum's comment. We have all been mates since James's family moved up here when we were in junior primary. Him and his family have even come camping out my community and my family has taken them out bush. We all know it's nothing about race between us. But even though he respected our culture, there was so much he just couldn't know.

'Those recruiters aren't likely to come looking up this way again anytime soon,' I say.

'Blow footy, they could be hurt out there!' Willum bites back, shooting me an accusing stare. 'Or bump into whoever the police are out looking for ...'

'Exactly! That's why they have *trained* police, firefighter volunteers and the ranger out there looking for them. Probably your uncles and that too. You guys can't do anything!' James answers. 'This might be our one big chance to make it with footy. When do recruiters or *anyone* from the real leagues ever come here? Why would they waste their time? I doubt they'll ever make this trip again. You'd be a dickhead to give that up, mate.'

'Yeah but those coppers are hopeless! They aren't from here, they don't know Country like us mob,' Willum argues. 'You putting too much faith in a handful of other people. This is big Country out here.'

'You boys have talent,' Brad adds. 'Let the police, firies and ranger do their jobs. You guys got to think of your future too. Be stupid to give up on your one big chance. Those year twelves will probably be found with a busted radiator or something. They'll just laugh hearing of you blokes running around looking for them.'

'We have to do something!' I almost shout in frustration. 'What if there is something more to old Henry's death? What if they are hurt? What if what we did actually did have something to do with it?'

I know what Brad is saying makes sense. People hit roos or get lost out of town all the time. I know the chance of that tyre holding until they were out of town was thin so we probably had nothing to do with them being late. I wonder if this new city principal and out-of-town cop have just blown it all out of proportion ... but then my gut instinct tells me otherwise. And that niggle in the back of my brain just won't quit. What dots am I not connecting? Willum pops his head around the corner of the bookshelf to check that the librarian isn't coming.

'I'll see what I can find out on the net? Maybe we can pass that onto the police to help or something?' James says, logging onto one of the library desktops. 'I'll check the satellite pictures, weather website to see if there is a chance they are just bogged after some rain ... Brad you jump on that other computer and search up tagged social media pics from our area to see if any tourists have accidentally snapped them in a pic, to narrow the search area.'

Willum and I eye each other. I am relieved that James has some kind of plan. Doing anything is better than nothing. But us mob don't find *real people* by sitting down on computers. I feel hopeless. I feel guilty. I feel stuck. I pace behind them while Willum stands with his arms crossed eyeing off the exit. It feels wrong just sitting around. The other boys are right though. This footy chance won't come up again and the bus will probably pull up any minute. I hold onto that like a life jacket. They will turn up any minute.

Frustrated, I walk over to the maps and history sections in our library. I quickly collect a small pile of books before sitting back down with my mates. *Small Town Histories, The Australian Atlas, Local Maps, Australian Bushwalking Guide.* Most of them were written a long time ago. I do find a map of this town and region in *Local Maps*: nothing new that I don't already know. I could probably even add a few things to this map that some out-of-town state planner wouldn't even dream existed here, like the old decommissioned town water tank that my mates and I sometimes swim in after a big rain. I wonder where I would hide if I had just murdered someone ... if that is what has happened. It's a big leap thinking old Henry's death is murder number one, even bigger thinking it is connected to the lost bus number two. I search the maps for routes out of town. There are three main roads, lots of back tracks the townie crew use to get around the township without having to bother driving through town. You'll often find people having a fire and a few beers on one of the back routes, or sitting down playing a card game under the trees. There's a few old beaten-up car bodies. Nice enough scenery and stuff out there though; some of the teacher mob use them as their afternoon walking tracks too. It wouldn't be too hard for someone to slip away ... to find another unsuspecting person to jump. My eyes follow the line of the river down the page and stop at a tight bend. That's where it happened. Strange that it is all as fresh as the day it happened. Guess this drama drags up the memories. Michael's brother overdosed there.

'Find the twelves yet?' Willum scoffs as he sits down next to me.

'Nah, brother,' I reply, addressing him the way our mob does. 'This whitefella map is like a little kid map with nothing on it!'

'Remember when old Aunty Shellene took us to this spot?' he points out another place he remembers. 'We had deadly fun running amuck down that dry riverbed. Was it you who nearly got bit by that big snake?'

'No way! That was you, or what?' I laugh it off. It feels like ages since we had been bush with the family. Back home in community I just hang out with my mates in the main street. That's one of the reasons Dad was happy to send me off for this football carnival. My mates and I had just been having fun, killing time when we broke into a few of the teachers' houses over the holidays. None of us are bad fellas though. Sometimes I just need action. If I am too still, sometimes a darkness creeps over me trying to drag me down. Other times, we are just bored, looking for something to do to get some excitement in our small community. Mostly we muck around but not always. Sometimes I have a rage that grows inside me, like the time that a new teacher said us mob shouldn't 'get handouts' and that she was going to teach us the 'proper way' to live. It had felt good throwing rocks on her roof and teasing her dog. Sometimes it's to just feel seen and heard like after the Government said they wanted to close our communities and, angry at the world, I had graffitied the shop walls and smashed some of the police station windows. Hear me, see me, I matter.

I bring my mind back to the present. I could use a little less drama right now though, crossing my fingers that the 12s will drive into the school carpark any moment. Looking at the map there was still heaps of gaps and this tourist map was only a fraction of the actual park.

'We wasting time though bro and you know it. We need to be out there. Let these two goofs play tech detectives. We could also be out there by now with the time we have wasted this morning. It's nearly ten. We should have grabbed those bikes as soon as we heard!' Willum whispers, making sure our friends don't hear.

I feel trapped. Maybe the other boys are right. The 12s will be found in no time and I'll have given up the chance to be noticed on the field. My big chance to get out of here. To live a life outside the outback.

'Argh!' Willum grunts, frustration clear on his face. 'Let's get some air, brother!'

The other two are deep in conversation about something they have found on the internet as we both slip outside.

4
DILEMMA

'We have to help them,' Willum says. My heart literally hurts with guilt at even putting my own football aspirations above the safety of the others on the bus. 'We need to find out what happened to them.'

'Brad is probably right. Old Henry just slipped and hit his head on a rock and drowned or something. The year twelves have nothing to do with it at all and are just broken down somewhere out bush. The cops will find them and bring them all back in no time and we'll look like idiots who jumped the gun and missed out on the recruiters,' I say. 'If none of the uncles have come grabbed us yet, nobody else has probably even gone out. Can't be that bad, hey?'

The words sound empty even as they pass through my lips.

Willum grabs his phone out of his pocket and checks if he has any missed calls or texts from our family. Nothing yet.

'You actually trust those outta town coppers to find that bus? They couldn't find the grey hairs coming out of their old man noses!' Willum urged. 'Those recruiter mob leave town first thing in the morning to head to Broome for the last match. We don't get a second chance with this. This footy thing means as much to me as it does to you, Dek.'

The bell rings, making me jump. This has been such an intense morning, I'm on edge.

Michael spots us out the front of the library as he walks past on the way to the oval. The police presence and search for our missing mob is bringing up painful memories of his brother's death for me, I can only imagine how he is feeling.

'So, what did you guys hear?' he asks, his eyes dark. 'Any news?'

'I am just glad to be out in the fresh air and allowed to talk without a teacher cutting us off,' Spencer joins us. 'This shit is pretty crazy, man! They are taking it all pretty seriously.'

'We cut class,' James says as he opens the door to exit the library.

'What? And you couldn't come grab us?' Michael growls, disappointment flashing across his face. He holds the almost forgotten ball in his hands, as we try to figure out the mystery of our missing mates.

'You know Ms Matthews would never let you guys out!' James snaps back in our defence.

'What did you guys find?' I ask James and Brad. We hadn't really talked in the library.

'I did find one pic tagged online from some tourists at a rest stop along the highway. They were having a break in the background. That was Monday, when they were driving into the park. Nothing else though,' James sounds flat. If anyone was going to find some missing digital footprint or track them online it was him. Sounds like that lead has gone cold.

'The weather has been hot, humid and dry in the build-up to the wet. The website said there was some heavy rainfall but that it was out around ranges outside the national park. They wouldn't have got more than a sprinkle. There were a few scrub fires around ... but no warnings or road closures on the national park website. They did have some wild dog warnings a few weeks back. I looked up on the year twelves' profiles as well. There wasn't any talk of anyone planning anything wild,' Brad added. If there was anything crazy planned Aaron would have told Willum anyway; those two hang out enough.

'They interrogated us all. Sounds like they don't have any strong leads yet,' Spencer says.

'I want to get out there!' I say feeling conflicted. They went camping out on *my* Country. 'I was thinking we might have messed something up on the bus that day we was mucking around. I would be dead if we'd caused anything to happen to that mob.'

'As if Dek,' Spencer scoffs, 'that was ages ago. Can't be, can it?'

Willum is on edge again, pacing as we talk. My own hands curl into tight fists, all the tension from the morning wanting to escape but with nowhere to go.

'Don't be stupid!' Brad says confidently. 'They'd have changed them long time ago. No way those tyres lasted this long. It's totally a breakdown or fuel or something. They'll be right. They'll find them soon.'

'Do you reckon they'll cancel the game tonight? We need to get out there,' Willum asks the rest of the boys, trying to give me an excuse to just abandon the game.

'I don't know. I heard the recruiters are scouting just this game then flying out on the mail plane first thing in the morning to watch one last game in Broome before they decide on the recruits,' Brad says slowly, weighing up the likelihood of a delay. 'In saying that, this is pretty serious, it's not like anyone is making it up as an excuse.'

'Yeah but they are on a schedule, you know? They need to get to the other game and make a decision in time for state representative competition. They have a whole region full of under-sixteens ready to take the opportunity anyway. And the comp won't impact the year twelves cause they are all older than sixteen,' Spencer says. I can tell he hates being the devil's advocate, the voice of reason.

'Who knows, we might find them broken down near one of your family spots? You know maybe that spring we always stop at on footy trips just out of town?' James tries to rationalise the situation again.

'Maybe,' I mumble.

'Dek, Aunty got any spare bikes?' Michael asks, his intense eyes so much like his brother's.

Michael isn't as good a player as Willum and I. I find myself bitter that he can just make the decision to dump the match that easily. Then again he knows the value of family and what happens when you lose someone you love.

'I'm in,' says Willum straight away.

'I want to ...' says James. 'I can't though. My mum would ground me for a month. Literally.'

'Ha you're fifteen, mate! You letting your mummy tell you what to do all the time?' I tease but I believe him. We all still owe our mothers respect. They grew us up.

James's mum banned him from going to the town pool for a month last summer when he didn't get back in time for dinner. My family had come into town for a funeral. It was a really hot summer and we'd stopped in to hang out with him on the way home from the pool. We thought his mum would give in after the first stinking hot weekend ... but she didn't. Getting grounded at fifteen would be big shame too!

'Mate, this footy thing could be my big break. The only way I'm gonna get out of this shitty town. I'm not brainy like you. I just can't,' Spencer says, unable to face us as he does. I know what he means; this footy opportunity would be everything for us mob too. You can get picked to attend an academy at sixteen and drafted into a club at seventeen so every little thing we can do now counts. That's big football contract money. A chance to set my family up. To travel the country. To break out of my life. Start afresh. You are only in your football prime for such a short time. I felt the same ... except for Brooklyn and Jenny. And with us mob, we've been raised in a culture where family comes first.

'Good idea anyway. You'll know where we are headed if we don't get back in time,' Willum gives the guys a break. He hasn't noticed that I haven't agreed yet.

5 THE CRASH

'I was just coming to find you!' Grandfather says to us, his face lighting up in relief as he walks around the corner from the office. He is talking in a mix of traditional language and Kriol that my brain quickly translates with ease. 'Some of your uncles are heading out bush. Those coppers are taking too long sitting on their hands. You and I are going to search one area while the rest of them mob look a few different spots.'

It's kind of a relief that something is finally happening. That the choice might be taken out of my hands. I try to think of how to tell Grandfather my worry.

‘It’s time you learnt how to track properly. None of this half-ass stuff you young fellas have been doing when we go out bush before,’ Grandfather is serious, his eyebrows are pulled into a tight line, head slightly bowed.

‘We were just heading out on our bikes anyway,’ Willum replies. ‘We were just going to ride out there and see if we could spot anything that the out-of-town cops might miss.’

‘Most of the cops are still fussing with that old station bloke. Or bothering us kids,’ Michael adds, spitting out the words like they taste bad. ‘Cause they haven’t got any firm leads, it sounds like they are just waiting it out to see if the bus just turns up!’

‘Hmmmm. Better we head out anyway. I’ve got a feeling we need to find them,’ Grandfather says, closing his eyes as if that helps him clarify this ‘feeling’ of his. ‘Not safe riding those highways on that little bush bike though. Best get back to your old Uncle Daniel camp to jump on with him. They could use your energy!’

‘I’ll jump on with you mob then,’ Michael says, face flushed with adrenaline ready to go.

‘Michael you can’t come, my grandson,’ Grandfather’s words hit Michael hard. His face curls up in an angry scowl. My cousin has never been good at hearing 'no' from Elders. 'Michael, your family just lost your big brother. They can't risk you out bush at a time like this.'

'Argh, I'm not a bloody kid!' Michael growls. 'Did Mum tell you I can't go?'

Michael automatically blames his mother. I guess I would in his shoes too. His mother has been really protective of Michael since that day. He isn't allowed out with us past seven at night and she's restricted what us fellas can do when we come around. She'd given up grog and turned to the church.

We all know the hurt of losing someone. The Government crunched some numbers and reckon us mob have lower life expectancy than other Australians and the highest suicide rates in the world. That happens when you invade someone's Country, have brutal conflicts with resistance fighters and have consequent policies that crush their spirits over 200 years I guess. Our way we can't even say Michael's brother's name out of respect. We are all related some way or another out here. We grew up running around after his big brother too. We know it will kill Michael to be left out.

'Come on, Grandfather. You can say that you needed him. He is almost a man now, doesn't need his mum giving him orders!' Willum appealed to Grandfather's authority as an Elder and the fact that Michael will be doing Law this summer.

Grandfather ignores Willum's plea and puts a hand on Michael's shoulder, 'Stay. Go back to your mother.'

Michael storms off towards his mother's house. I know there will be a big blue when he gets there. He won't take no for an answer. But his mum is a tough old lady too. She was stolen and only found her way back to Country a few years before Michael was born. She'd lived through a lot. We all knew better than to cross her. Usually. Since Michael's big brother had died, things had been different though. Michael had changed.

Grandfather turns to me and my remaining mates and nods back towards the carpark.

'I'll catch him up,' says Spencer, turning to run after Michael. 'You coming Willum?'

I'm feeling annoyed. Spencer didn't wait around to have time for Grandfather to talk him into coming. Spencer was family too.

'I can't Grandfather,' my mouth dry as I choke out the words, knowing this could be my fault and that I owe it to them to be out there helping. 'I won't be any help to you anyway. And we promised coach we wouldn't let him down with this recruiter thing. He didn't have to let me on the team at such late notice.'

'You might have a different insight on the tracks I follow. You gifted – that special sense passed down to you,' Grandfather says. 'Plus, you've got better hearing and eyesight than me these days.'

I want to help. If there was any way at all I'd contributed to this whole messed-up scenario, I owed it to my cousin, and to Jenny. Culture way we are meant to listen to our Elders. It's just I don't think there is much we can do to help out Grandfather any more than he could do himself. Plus there is the pretty big chance that this is just a series of accidents and that the police will rule Henry's death accidental and the bus will come driving in any minute now. Hope. I cling to it.

Grandfather had the 'sense' too. Our people say it's black magic. We both get feelings about things. Know things other people don't.

'You're the last one here,' Grandfather states, 'other than this mob who wouldn't know their own footprints from a camel's. No offence.'

James laughs holding up his foot. The laughter sounds weird today.

Guilt fills my body. I was always taught don't choose anything over family.

I look past him into the troopy. My boots and our bags are already sitting on the back seat. Do I tell him the very reason I want to rush out there? Or that part of me fears finding out that I had something to do with it and finding the bus might just confirm that fear? Or that a little selfish part of me just really, really wants to make my family proud and make something out of football. These opportunities are so rare out here in the bush.

'Your mum packed snacks for the road,' Grandfather gives me a sly smile, noticing my gaze. He knows I don't really have a choice.

'This is our Country,' my Grandfather says slowly, looking out past the houses into the distance. His head is tilted and his eyes shine. I can tell he is thinking deeply about our ancestors, our culture, our history. He has long told me about the connection our people have with this land. 'Police backup from the other towns won't be here straight away ... and they have all that heavy gear that will weigh them down, and procedures that will stop them listening to the land and using their instincts. The year twelves deserve everyone they can to help them. It's hot.

And the land is unpredictable. They might not have much time.'

'Grandfather I gave my word,' I'm not sure why I'm trying to talk my way out of it. Usually I would give anything to be out there in the drama at a time like this. To help Brook and Jenny. To make up for not being there, the sober one, the night Michael's brother died. This match is just so big.

'I understand how much this football thing means to you, Dek. That's why I took you into town and have stayed around to support you,' Grandfather says gently, then his tone changes. 'It's just your uncles didn't want to take me in case my old bones slow them down. Bloody bastards forgot who raised them up and taught them everything out bush. I've just got a feeling that this mob are missing out deep in Country. I don't think your uncles will find them.'

My mind is spinning. I'm so torn. I want to be out there helping. But now the only way to do it is to travel with Grandfather. Grandfather truly believes we have the skills to match modern technology out in the bush. Now I'm second-guessing us all together; I just can't see how an old man and a teenager could find something that the police and ranger couldn't. Especially if his own sons didn't believe in him.

'We'll bring the twelves home,' Grandfather comforts my other mates. 'And you mob can help back here. Keep digging and keep us updated too.'

'Can you guys explain it to coach?' I say, trying to cover all my bases in case I'm not back in time. 'Might get a break since it looks like it's official police business?'

'Yeah, mate,' James agrees.

'Right then, let's go,' adrenaline pumps through my body, decision made.

Walking over towards the troopy I notice the driver, Officer Thomas, sitting in the driver's seat, eyes forward, tapping impatiently on the steering wheel. My mood squashed as quickly as it had come.

'Why is he here?' I turn to ask my grandfather. I thought he had borrowed the troopy from Uncle Mark or Jeff. Grandfather's beaten-up Holden wouldn't make it far off the highway. I am surprised any time it even gets us to town and back. Any time we had been out bush from town one of my uncles had let us jump on with them.

'Your uncles needed them troopies to take the rest of them lot out looking. I've got a feeling they are looking in the wrong areas, so I needed to get out there no matter what,' a twinkle in his eye tells me he knows I sense it too. 'I've got a feeling about this.'

I sigh but keep my head down as I climb in the back. I feel my jaw clench in frustration but clip in the seatbelt. Driving out on the straight highway, the UHF radio is already busy with reports from all the search parties. Everyone checking in and giving updates. It helps distract me from the awkward tension I'm feeling in the car.

'We just been into la swimming spot at five mile. *Minyon*, nothing there.' The radio crackles as Uncle Daniel checks in. 'Heading out the first river crossing to track around next. Over.'

'Heading straight out la camp,' Grandfather replies. 'Keep us updated. Over.'

We also get some of the updates that our family wouldn't be hearing on normal UHF channels. The police use a digital radio network that's encrypted; so criminals can't hear them I suppose. I remember when they changed cause my Uncle Daniel had sworn like a trooper when his radio scanner stopped picking up their old channels. He isn't a criminal but he sure liked getting a heads up about which cops were out doing random breath checks around town. I'd been at the shops with him one afternoon soon after the switch, in town for some reason or another, and he'd bumped into one of the long-time cops off duty. They'd had a yarn and Uncle had jokingly complained that he couldn't catch the local police gossip any more. The officer laughed along with him but complained how the new system still had its limits out bush too in valleys or deep bush or storms or fires. He'd said it was about bloody time they got the new tech though – the city cops had had it for ages before they'd decided to budget it into the upgrades in some country towns.

'HC104 this is HC107, do you copy?'

'This is Officer Thomas HC104. Go ahead,' Officer Thomas responds.

'Four one five highway fifty ks from town. Investigating,' the radio comes through clearly.

'En route,' Officer Thomas responds.

'Yeah roger that, brother,' Uncle Jeff continues on the normal UHF channels unaware of the police communication. 'We checking la tourist camp spot with that barbeque and toilet block. Over.'

Grandfather motions to the policeman for the handset.

'Got it, Jeff,' Grandfather presses the button to respond.

‘Hey fellas. Us truckies have been hearing the news on the channel all morning. We’ve been passing info down the line and will let you know if we spot anything. Over,’ a truck driver overhearing the chatter responds. It’s pretty quiet on the road today.

After half an hour it becomes background noise. I spend the trip remembering back to my time out bush with my Elders, trying to think of all the lessons they taught me. I remember swimming in cool waterholes so deep you couldn’t touch the bottom. I remember fishing with my cousins. I remember eating sweet sugarbag bush honey. I feel ashamed that I haven’t been out bush for a long time. Every time my old people went out since I’ve been in high school, I’ve had something else to do: a football match, the pool with my mates, playing computer games or a party with the boys.

It had been one of those parties back home on community where I’d seen Jenny. She’d come back with her family from town one weekend to visit her sick grandmother. She’d looked deadly in tight jeans and a basketball jersey. Bulls. My favourite team. She is promised to someone of the right skin, our cultural way. Not that many people still stick to that these days. We aren’t the right skin so I wasn’t supposed to have any feelings for her. The boys and I had been drinking and dancing the way we all do. I'd gone outside to try to get some phone reception – you can only get it in a few places around our community. She'd been there too ...

We can't be more than fifty kilometres south of town when the troopy slows, pulling me from my memories.

'Why are we stopping?' I ask a little dazed as I look out my side window.

Police traffic cones block the road near a large drop off. My heart sinks at the thought that my cousin and Jenny might be down there. Will Grandfather be the one to tell Brooklyn and Jenny's parents what happened if we find them dead?

'Were you asleep this whole time?' Officer Thomas scoffs. 'Officer Sweeney just called this in for backup. She's called in the flying doctors.'

My heart leaps and I quickly take off my seatbelt. My hand is on the door handle, 'Let's get down there!'

'Wait, Dek,' Grandfather orders, opening his door. I'm already out and rushing towards the edge when I feel Grandfather's hand on my shoulder. 'We've got to do it all properly and quickly so no one else gets busted up in the rescue.'

'Have a sniff around, see if you can be any help,' Officer Thomas moves around to our side of the vehicle a little way off. His harsh tone snaps me out of my frustration with my grandfather. What does he think we are, bloody sniffer dogs? My grandfather doesn't seem to notice, he nods, his mouth in a tight, thin line. Why had this copper even agreed to take us out just to treat the old man like that?

There are dark skid marks on the road. Officer Sweeney is consulting with a handful of volunteer firefighters; some are unpacking their equipment from their troopy and consulting a map. She gives my grandfather a respectful wave. She's been in town for a few years and has a good relationship with Elders and locals.

It's clear that someone ran off the road. Grandfather bends down to touch the burnt rubber, sniffing it and measuring its width with his hands. He gazes out over the valley, then looks up and down the road that runs along the cliff. I follow his gaze, subconsciously scanning for anyone suspicious hiding along the roadside.

Grandfather stops just by the edge of the cliff, looking at a faint skid mark there. I look over the edge into the thick bush below. It's lucky Officer Sweeney even noticed the faint trail of smoke spiralling up.

Her experience attending scenes like this must have played a part in her sharp eye. The skid marks on the road wouldn't necessarily have been that obvious to her travelling 110 kilometres on the highway out here. I try to visualise a way down. The quickest route might be to travel along the road a bit, climb down the crumbling rock face and then trek back.

'Get back in the car, we are done here,' Grandfather states flatly, turning around and passing back through the police barrier with me on his heels, shocked.

'What? We didn't even go down?' I protest. If I'm out here I damn well want to make sure everyone is safe. Now the old man has just changed his mind. 'I'm not bloody going anywhere till they are safe.'

I turn to head down the road as I had been planning. Grandfather grabs me tight on the shoulder and spins me around. I feel my body tense and rage building. I'm not a little kid to be pulled around.

'We are no help here,' he replies solemnly, letting his hand drop from my shoulder to his side. His voice serious and sad. 'That's not the bus. But even if it is, the cops have already found them and we are no use here.'

'How do you know it's not the bus?' I ask, relief washing over me. How can he know that when the police obviously think otherwise?

‘The tyre marks aren’t wide enough or deep enough. A loaded bus with kids and bags would have made worse skids than that,’ the old man reasons. I am a little impressed. But if this is not the bus, *where* are they?

‘This is two cars,’ Grandfather adds with a frown. ‘The second one didn’t even have time to brake. It looks like it was run off the road.’

‘Where you two going?’ Officer Thomas huffs over, frustration etched deep in the lines of his face.

‘This isn’t the kids,’ Grandfather says carefully. ‘We need to head to the camp site.’

‘Mate,’ Officer Thomas spits out, implying anything but the meaning of the word, ‘we can’t just leave the scene of an accident based just on your word.’

My grandfather explains his conclusions to the Officer. I can tell my grandfather is irritated at having to justify himself, just a subtle twitch of his eye that I have learnt to watch out for when he is annoyed with me. My grandfather is accustomed to covering up his true feelings with white officials though. Grandfather grew up when Aboriginal people weren’t even classified as ‘people’ according to the Constitution. I watch Officer Thomas’s face as Grandfather’s explanations continue. His eyebrows slowly creep up his face in amazement at the quick conclusions my grandfather has drawn.

'Sergeant O'Neil asked you to take me where I needed to go,' my grandfather says finally and firmly. 'Would you like to radio him and check?'

That explains it. Sergeant O'Neil has been in town for a few years now running the police station. He respected our Elders as guides and trackers in the lost tourist incident last year, which consolidated his trust in their opinions. I knew him from the times he had driven out our way to support incidents out in the communities. While he was rigid to the word of the law, even when it didn't quite fit our remote context or clashed with Aboriginal Law, I'm pretty sure he was well respected by my grandfather also. Fair and consistent if nothing else.

Officer Thomas's cheek muscles spasm as he clenches his jaws thinking through his next move.

'Officer Sweeney has the SES firefighters here, and the emergency helicopter is on its way,' he says as if the idea to leave was his. 'We'll keep an eye out for the school bus as we drive out.'

Officer Thomas has a quick word to his colleague as we walk back to the troopy. So many thoughts are running through my brain as I watch the Officer walk back towards us. My train of thought is interrupted by a loud screeching and suddenly a car speeds around the corner.

'Stay in there,' Officer Thomas growls as the other car slams to a halt by the police barrier.

'NOOO!' screams a woman as she stumbles out of the car. Her eyes wide, arms flailing, she looks around wildly. Her eyes lock with mine, wild, raw.

6
RANGER

My heart skips with fear as I look around in the direction the woman has just sped up from.

'You monster,' she screams again, pulling a hand free to point to me. I spin around in the troopy, half expecting to see a murderer creeping up behind us or some monster climbing over the troopy.

Office Thomas grabs her long before she reaches us and holds her in a bear hug until the other officer comes to help. Grandfather turns to me in the back.

'What's that about?' Grandfather asks. 'Do you know her?'

'I have no bloody idea,' I reply. We watch from the window, intrigued, as the police bundle the woman into the passenger seat of Officer Sweeney's car. Officer Sweeney turns on the car and leaves her in the aircon, her body leaned over, head in hands. The two officers have a quick conversation, backs to us. Officer Thomas returns shaking his head. He starts the troopy and begins driving. We wait patiently for an update that doesn't come.

'What was going on there, mate?' Grandfather asks, turning down the radio to get the policeman's full attention.

'Turns out we *were* on the wrong track with that lead,' Officer Thomas starts. 'That lady was expecting her husband back this morning from a buck's party camping. She used her GPS tracker on his smartphone, which led her to the crash site.'

Grandfather nods. I sit amazed; he had been right. It wasn't the school bus after all. If her husband's car had crashed much further out of town, his wife would have had no way to track him down; reception drops out not long down the road.

'She thought your young fella was locked up in the back and had something to do with it,' Officer Thomas laughed. 'More likely her husband was just drunk from the night before.'

I don't think it's funny. It's a racist assumption to

think that if a blakfella is near a crime, they must be involved. Clearly the policeman has no issue with this perception.

Grandfather's head slumps and shakes, 'It's a sad thing. Our community jumping to assumptions and blame without the whole story.'

The policeman scoffs and turns up the radio again. We drive on in silence broken by the occasional update. Even our mob are still checking in sometimes. Now only Uncle Jeff is still in reception and he hasn't found them out around town at the close swimming spots; nobody has found them at some of the tourist rest stops along the way. Most of the handful of police are still canvassing around the cattle station for their evidence and suspects. I pull my phone out of my pocket, push my earphones in to drown out the dangerous thoughts swimming through my mind. I'm not getting any reception so I just listen to the songs I have downloaded. My grandfather and I are both used to these long drives. This long straight highway is the same one we drive on to get out to community.

We pass only a truck and a few caravans for most of the trip. Grey nomads they call them. Old people who save up all their lives to buy fancy caravans, better than my whole house, and then travel around out bush before they die. Or something like that. Good on 'em I reckon if that's what they want to do. I've never seen a blakfella doing it that way though. My grandfather can't afford to upgrade his shit-box car let alone buy a caravan even though he has been working hard all his life. Or most of his life at least. Grandfather has told me how equal pay didn't even come in till the late sixties or early seventies and that many station owners just kicked the blakfellas off their stations instead of paying them fairly. Grandfather had been involved in the land rights movement in the early seventies so that didn't do him any favours getting work again at that time. A rage spreads through my body every time I think about the way he'd been treated though. Think he deserves a bloody mansion for the amount of shit him and our mob had to put up with. Makes me mad when whitefellas just say it wasn't them or not their fault. It wasn't but my grandfather deserves the respect to be heard, listened to, believed ... maybe even helped a little now he's in his old age dealing with the scars of all that time.

We pass another caravan. Makes sense to see a few in a row. They seem to travel in convoys, making friends along the way. There isn't many of the grey nomads at this time of year though. They mostly come up in the middle of the dry when it's not too hot and humid.

'Turn off here,' my grandfather points his lips towards a small sealed road that turns to gravel before winding off into the bush. It looks vaguely familiar.

'That's not the way into the park,' Officer Thomas shakes his head, driving past the road and carrying on. 'Let's just stick to what we know, hey?'

'That's the back road in,' Grandfather replies. 'Turn around.'

The landscape has changed, burnt black. Charcoaled tree trunks, round patches of charred spinifex, parts of the road still molten. It kind of matches the dark tone these two up front are using with each other.

'Pull over,' my grandfather commands. Officer Thomas's whole body stiffens. He continues driving for a few metres in defiance and then pulls over too quick onto dirt, sending the troopy skidding with a thump into the low branches of a tree by the road. He glares at my grandfather. Staring him down. In our culture, you don't really talk looking each other in the eye. When yarning with any of us mob it's the polite thing to talk looking at something else, or standing side by side not front on. Looking into each other's eyes when you are talking is a sign of disrespect or challenge. That's what this is. My grandfather returns his gaze.

'Look, mate. I've got better places to be,' Officer Thomas growls. 'We have a potential murder, a double crash and missing students. And I'm stuck out here babysitting you two. We don't have the resources for this shit. I'll be damned if we have to go walkabout any more than we already are!'

'Sergeant O'Neil ordered you to take me where I needed,' Grandfather says, keeping his tone neutral. 'We need to go in back that way.'

'That teacher wouldn't have driven out that way,' Officer Thomas softens his tone, knowing Grandfather is right. His body still tense.

'There's a heap of reasons they would change their way in. This fire looks fresh enough; maybe Ms Pritchard was too cautious to drive on further through the flames and went in the back way? Maybe my granddaughter convinced her to stop at a few waterholes down that way,' Grandfather explains. 'I've just got a feeling.'

Officer Thomas looks in his rear-view mirror, considering the situation. 'She hadn't written in the school documents the exact route she was taking in, just that they planned on camping at the "public camp site" and that she had a few sites she was going to visit from there. She wasn't very specific. Think Ms Wilson has something to answer for approving that camp as well.'

'Look, fella,' Grandfather says, voice slightly tightening. I can tell he has had enough of talking. 'Even you have to admit there is a good chance they are still actually in the park. If it hadn't been for that crash, most of that mob would be out here helping look too.'

'Argh!' Officer Thomas slams his fist down on the steering wheel in frustration, takes a deep breath and turns the troopy around. 'We can't rule anything out. There are still plenty of places being checked closer to town.'

We turn off into the national park. Officer Thomas jumps out to let some air out of the tyres to avoid getting bogged in the ever changing dirt road. The road changes along the way from a bumpy dirt track to loose dirt stretches that send us fishtailing and to damp riverbeds where the sides have been eroded away.

'Looks like they got some decent rain that way,' Grandfather motions towards our home community way. 'Might have flash flooded downstream here.'

I hope he is right. That they have just been washed off the road a bit and are bogged. We can collect them up and head back. Although we all know how deadly flooded roads can be. This is the Australian outback where you can have a fire burning in one spot and rain just over the range. The land of 'drought and flooding rains' as Dorothea Mackellar put it.

'Better check in with our new location,' Officer Thomas grumbles, his anger at being overruled again by my grandfather barely disguised under his flat features. He grabs the UHF handset and radios in.

'Base this is HC104, do you copy?'

The UHF crackles in reply. 'Bloody useless.'

Officer Thomas drives one-handed as he checks his phone, 'Nothing. Are you getting any?'

I shake my head, 'There won't be any mobile reception out this way.'

'Hell, now I'm off road in the bloody outback without updating the station,' Officer Thomas grows, bad mood building. 'You better be right about this old man.'

'What's our plan?' I ask to break the tension that is thick in the air.

'Keep an eye out this way. I've just got a feeling,' Grandfather is interrupted as Officer Thomas scoffs.

'Stop here,' Grandfather commands as we approach an old shack. The main tourist centre is closer to the entrance of the park. This shack looks run-down. Although knowing how many tourists they get out here during peak season, I wouldn't be surprised if they had to use it then.

'This used to be the main ranger station back when you were a kid, Dek,' Grandfather pointed towards the hut. 'We used to take you and your dad out this way sometimes.'

Jumping out from the back of the troopy I walk around to the bull bar and stretch using the steel to pull my arms out straight. I notice the antenna for the radio is snapped sideways. Might be the reason for the poor reception. Officer Thomas pushes past me and walks inside. I feel adrenaline rushing through my body and my hands clench. The way you treat people is everything in our culture and this officer is just rubbing me up the wrong way. Grandfather notices my body language and puts a hand on my shoulder.

'Let's just leave all that for later, hey?' he says, voice even and calm. 'Let's just find our mob.'

I take a big breath and nod. Grandfather keeps his hand gently on my shoulder as we walk inside. There is nobody here. Cobwebs hang from the windows. Officer Thomas looks over some dusty maps spread out on the table. My grandfather looks through the cupboard at the back. The bottom drawers have labels that are faded and peeling. His fingers trace some of the items: an old UHF box, books, tins and bones, sending dust flying in the strips of light let in through the little holes in the roof.

Looking out the dirty window, I try to remember coming out here as a kid like Grandfather had said. If I ever go out with family now it's usually just out to our family block or to the local waterholes. I haven't been out for a good while.

I do remember a while back, the ranger here had been embroiled in some scandal with animal trafficking or something, but they could never prove anything. We've got some unique animals that are apparently worth something to rich international people. I was actually a little curious to meet the sneaky dude; he never really showed his face around town much since that drama.

An old ranger opens the door and steps inside. He isn't surprised to see us; he must have seen our troopy. I wonder if Officer Thomas has radioed ahead although the ranger wouldn't have known to meet us here. Maybe they have called in an Aboriginal ranger to coordinate the search this side of the park. His eyebrows are grey above his dark brown eyes, his leathery skin is old and wrinkled. I briefly wonder why they don't just get this old man to do the tracking, but from the deep lines on his dark brown forehead I figure he must be way older than Grandfather. He must have been doing this job for a long time. He walks in barefoot. He must have left his boots by the door, though I don't see them as he comes inside. Probably an old habit, maybe like my old grandmother who would spend hours scrubbing the floor from the old times when she had to make her room spotless in the children's home. I feel bad as I look at the mud I have tracked inside, although it does seem to blend in with the dust on the floor. The old ranger leaves his dusty old bandana resting over his mouth and his ranger hat low over his eyes. I nod my head, dropping my eyes, in greeting. Grandfather walks over head down as a sign of respect and shakes his hand.

'You must be Mick's native sidekick then?' Officer Thomas says, matter-of-factly, by way of greeting. I watch the ranger's eyes for signs of offence at the policeman's rudeness of calling him a 'native' and not addressing him with the respect worthy of an Elder. 'I was just looking at this map trying to figure out where we are. Does that UHF box work? Even my police radio's not getting a signal.'

The old ranger shrugs and makes no move to check. He is resting his shoulders against the doorframe, eyes alert watching us. I'm not sure I would give the Officer the time of day or an explanation either. Grandfather starts to walk over to check the radio, but Officer Thomas waves him away.

'We've got a murderer on the loose, a crash, missing teens ... and no contact with the police. Gosh I hate the outback,' Officer Thomas mutters as he fiddles with the knobs on the UHF.

Grandfather stands with me by the window, bemused look on his face, as we watch the Officer fussing over the box.

'You from around here, brother?' Grandfather asks, looking beyond the ranger out the door as a sign of respect. There is something different in Grandfather's body language that I just can't place. The ranger flicks his hand behind him in our sign language way, meaning from back that way. Officer Thomas hits his fist on the old UHF box, making me jump and stopping all conversation.

'Bloody things,' Officer Thomas cuts in. 'Any parts around here?'

The Officer doesn't wait for a reply. He begins rummaging through some of the drawers at the bottom of the cupboard. 'Grab this.'

Grandfather takes the small emergency pack from his hands and takes it to the table in the middle of the room to have a look through: radio, flares, first aid, water, an old park map and dried food.

Officer Thomas continues to pile stuff on the floor around him.

I'm more interested in watching my grandfather as he repacks the emergency pack. His eyes regularly flick from the pack to the old ranger. He looks puzzled.

'All I want is some bloody fuses!' Officer Thomas growls in frustration as he continues to rummage through the cupboard. I think he is a bit flustered to be on a back road without checking in with one of those officers. His anxiety makes me anxious to get out and look for the bus. We are wasting time in here. I tap Grandfather on the shoulder and motion for him to go outside. Grandfather must be thinking the same thing and moves to follow me without hesitation, emergency pack in hand. I walk past the ranger head down. He doesn't move from his position on the doorframe as we walk by.

'Let's get a head start,' I say, walking towards the troopy. 'Ranger can give him a lift down that way when he's done fiddling with that thing.'

'Are you suggesting we steal a police troopy?' Grandfather's tone sounding more amused than like he is trying to deter me. I'd 'borrowed' a car before, not that I'd tell Grandfather that. I look around but can't see the ranger's four-wheel drive. He must have parked it up the road a bit.

'I just have a feeling we need to hurry up. I don't feel like justifying myself to that cop again,' I say quietly but I don't need to convince him; Grandfather is already in the front seat. He throws the emergency pack over his shoulder onto the back seat.

'Gee, Grandfather, I don't know how you can be so strong,' I say, climbing in as Grandfather turns the key in the ignition. 'I don't know how you didn't get wild with that copper.'

'You don't change people like that with conflict and words, Dek,' Grandfather replies, setting off down the road. 'You got to show them with actions; you got to rise above.'

'Or steal their car?' I laugh, turning around in time

to see the Officer's face as he steps out the door. We turn the bend too quickly before I can finish lapping up the moment.

'We didn't steal it, Dek,' Grandfather said, a slight smile flicking across his lips. 'He can have it back as soon as he hurries up and helps us look for these missing mob.'

The road looks like it is occasionally used, deep ditches created along the tyre marks from repeated use. We pass a few thin side tracks and turn right at a fork in the road. It's hard to talk over the noise as the troopy bumps along the corrugated road.

Grandfather slows and moves the troopy into high-range gear to get through a deep, muddy riverbed. My heart sinks when I feel the tyres spin. I watch for Grandfather's reaction out of the corner of my eye.

'Jump out Dek and have a look,' he says matter-of-factly. Getting bogged out bush is nothing new.

I jump down into the mud, feeling my feet sink to the ankles. I try and see which tyre is having the trouble. I kick the one closest to me. Officer Thomas had done a shit job of letting the air out. No wonder we were bogged. The niggling feeling in my stomach starts up again. The tyres remind me of the dumb prank we'd pulled, that I might be responsible. I feel like throwing up. Did we have time to let the tyres down, chuck branches under them or dig us out a bit? Did we have time to set up the snatch strap even if we did have a decent-sized tree to attach it to? I let out a few swear words about the cop before pulling open the door again to fill my grandfather in.

'The idiot hardly let down the tyres,' I spit. 'It'll take us a while to get her out.'

Grandfather stares down the road, hands tight on the wheel. With a deep breath he jumps out his side and walks around to inspect the tyres too.

'We can't mess around with the troopy, Grandfather,' I say, determined that we keep moving. 'The ranger can pull it out with a winch or snatch strap when they pull up here soon.'

'You're right,' Grandfather agrees. 'The camp site is less than fifteen minutes walk up the road now. They can catch up.'

I slip the emergency pack into my backpack and pull it onto my back. Grandfather pulls his on with a grunt. The road is no easier to walk on than drive – road covered in rocks just the right size to twist an ankle soon turns into 'bulldust', light and sucky sand, to wet and muddy in the creek beds that run over the track, to uneven compact dirt.

I'm glad when we turn a bend and see the camp site ahead. I look around: a cleared dirt circle about the size of our school oval with a short fence all around, a drop dunny off to one side and fire pit with barbeque plate in the middle. It looks the same as any camp ground I have ever seen ... and more interestingly, it's empty and overgrown.

Grandfather walks to the perimeter looking for clues. I follow, kicking the soft red dirt with my shoe and wondering how long until Officer Thomas catches up ... and what will happen when he does. A sharp pain shoots up my leg.

'Argh!' I yell, flicking off a couple of large insects. 'Bloody bull ants!'

I look around to see the ground is crawling with them and stomp on as many as I can. I might be the only blakfella with an ant allergy. Insect bites swell up like marbles.

'Get out of the nest, you idiot!' Grandfather warns, pulling my arm away. He sits me down further away and scans the bush again. Finding what he looks for he chews a leaf and spits the mushy pulp onto my leg. The sticky mess starts to numb my leg.

'Should take the sting out,' he says, 'You're going to have to just walk it off ... we need to get back to looking.'

He motions for me to get the water out of the pack and swills it around his mouth to clean the bush medicine out. As I bend down to rub my leg I notice the tiny ant hills are scattered all over the camp site. Grandfather taps me on the head with the water bottle.

'Come on, kid. Enough mucking around, hey?'

I blush with embarrassment. Stepping on ants' nests is a total city slicker rookie mistake. I'm so on edge at the moment I'm not being my usual self. I need to focus.

I wince with pain but follow behind him again. Watching where I'm walking carefully. Grandfather squats down, gently sifts the dirt between his fingers. Holding it up, he lets the dirt fall to the ground, blowing softly. He presses his fingertips into the dirt. Standing up, he looks around the camp site.

'What did the ancestors tell you today, Grandfather?' I ask, not managing to hide my mocking tone. Grandfather either doesn't notice or he pretends that he doesn't.

'I was feeling the properties of the dirt here, Grandson. How the dirt holds marks, if it is wet from rain, if it will easily blow away in the wind. How much we can trust the marks we will find here – how long they have been here or how quickly they may have been covered. The land has much to share with those who are willing to be silent, observe and listen.'

I feel a little ashamed at my attempts to mock him. I have not respected this knowledge. He always used to take us out bush and tells us Creation stories, and even though I know he got called out for tracking, I'd just assumed that meant finding footprints and walking around until you found whoever you were looking for! We could all follow a goanna back to its hole in my family ... I just didn't realise that dirt could tell us so much.

He walks the camp site again while I stand back against a tree waiting. I am relieved that the sting in my leg has dulled to a low ache. I wonder why Officer Thomas hasn't hooned around the bend yet. I can totally picture him ranting and raving to the ranger as they drive here. I'm kind of looking forward to the confrontation. Grandfather knows how to hold his own. And I'm not afraid to tell that copper what I think too.

I haven't seen any tracks other than dingos or feral dogs. Grandfather stops silently to look around, his head tilted to the side, eyes squinting, mouth drawn in a sharp line. Outwardly looking for the physical clues, inwardly listening to his intuition, his cultural experience.

Leaves whisper. Twigs crack. Birds call. Sounds I have heard many times out bush. Grandfather steps into the vegetation. The knot in my stomach grows. I feel like he has found the right direction ... and I feel like I should go the other way. Today, in the full midday sun, the sounds I have heard every day of my life have never sounded more foreboding. Are they masking the hiss of a burst radiator? The groans of an injured student? The sound of my dying family? Concealing a murderer's footfalls? Are they hiding the growls of monsters? Now I'm not a wimp. I'd happily camp out bush with my mates or take on the biggest guy on the footy field. I just can't shake this strange feeling. I hesitate.

'Shouldn't we wait for Officer Thomas and the ranger?' I ask. I'd been the one rushing to get out here but now I falter. My stomach turns at the thought of looking for the others without backup. 'He can't be too far away.'

'Dek,' my grandfather says slowly, looking back at me. He is taking his time to find each word. 'I have a feeling we need to find them. They might not have much time. Not enough time to deal with that cop.'

'Me too,' I can't deny I feel the same. 'Can't we just drive a path with it through the scrub when they get here though?'

'I think the cop will forgive me for our little head start,' Grandfather motions to the boulders, hills and thicker trees. 'I can't track properly in a troopy anyway. It'll be good to have a look around on foot before they catch up.'

We always bush bash through scrub back home. I'm worried we will take too long by foot ... and that it will be harder for Officer Thomas and the ranger to find us.

The knowledge that my football match starts at 6pm ... and that Jenny could be injured out there ... drives me to step forward. I have a feeling my life will be changed forever either way. Maybe I should just follow the old man and get this over with. The quicker we find them the quicker I am back on the field. Still, I'm not eager to be looking for them without any backup.

'What are you afraid of?' Grandfather replies. 'We are going in with the knowledge of our ancestors, fully aware of what monsters are in there.'

7

BUSH

'Monsters?' I ask with a shaky voice. I haven't been afraid of boogeyman stories since primary school. Grandfather used to tell us but us mob out bush grow up knowing about black magic and spiritual stuff all around us. Standing here about to step out into the unknown without backup, with my growing sense of danger, I'm nervous.

'Well, a whole class of kids don't just go missing without a trace on their own, do they?' Grandfather replies. 'You know about our monsters from blakfella way.'

'There are a million ways to get lost out here,' I brush off Grandfather's comment. I'm not going to let the old man get under my skin. And yet suddenly I am aware of just how isolated and alone we are. Half of me wants to think it's just myths and fantasy like the teachers at school said when I'd been scared of them on school camp in grade 4. Growing up Aboriginal in the bush though, someone in everyone's family has seen one or been affected by black magic or knows the magic men. Lots of my family are Christian too from the mission days and those pastors always preach demons and Satan that sound awfully like our stories. To lots of our mob they aren't just myths; they could be as real as the birds flitting in the trees. Part of me wants it to be a monster of old, that way it can't have been because of me and our stupid prank with the bus. 'That's olden day stories. Out deep in the bush, not here?'

'I guess we'll find out, won't we?' Grandfather says flatly. 'Let's find these kids before it gets dark!'

Grandfather walks further into the thick bush. I hesitate by the edge of the campground. I look back. The policeman is nowhere to be seen yet. He can't be too far out. Maybe they took the wrong fork in the road? Maybe he got a call back to the other accident? Maybe they got the radio working and heard that the students had been found somewhere else? Maybe he is just sitting having a good old yarn with the ranger. Should we stay here and wait?

A feral dog howls in the distance. Birds in a nearby tree fly up shocked by our noise. A feather floats down and brushes my cheek. I walk in quickly after my grandfather.

I'd been out hunting in the bush with my family before. I'm not usually afraid of walking around in the wild. But today is different. This place is different.

When I catch up to Grandfather, he is hunched over a small bush, examining one leaf in his hand. I know a little about tracking so I scan the bushes for clues of my own. I look for tracks, for twigs snapped, evidence that anyone has been this way. He rises slowly, licking his finger and testing the breeze. He shakes his head.

'I can't find a track again,' he says, pointing in one direction. He begins walking steadily, each foot placed carefully as he studies the environment around us.

'How do you know to go this way then?' I ask, knowing well enough to trust his instincts but worried at the same time. We don't have time to waste getting lost or chasing a false trail. I have this match to get back to and a limited window to make it back in time ... and if the year 12s are hurt ... if Jenny is hurt ... I push the thought from my mind.

'I've got a feeling. Like a hand of a compass moving in my belly. This tingling sense that they are out this way. This is our Country. I trust our ancestors will guide us to find our lost blood,' Grandfather replies, raising his eyebrows. I feel it too. 'And when have you ever known me to get lost out bush?'

'Yeah, well, this is different, I can feel it,' I can't quite explain the feeling. Something isn't right out here. I haven't been out this way for a long time. On Country closer to home I know all my landmarks and have a good feeling which way things are from each other. Out here I'm trusting my grandfather and my instinct.

Grandfather stops and turns to me. He grabs me by the shoulders and holds me still.

'Stop. Look around you. Listen,' he commands. I listen carefully trying to make sense of the sounds. I look around at the distant hills, the thick scrub. 'This is our Country. We will find them.'

'I know. I've just got a bad feeling,' I argue, frustration making my hands ball into fists. I know the hunting sounds to look for and the sound of waterfalls in the distance, all the things you hear back home closer to community and our favourite places. This is still our Country but I don't know it like the way I do back home. I wish I knew the songlines like Grandfather to lead us to that mob.

'The sun, moss on trees and the stars show us direction. Our songlines guide us through our Country,' Grandfather soothes, letting go of my shoulder and moving forward through the bush again humming. 'I know the bush sounds: the sounds of the animals gathered around a waterhole, what the bush sounds like when it is alarmed, all the animal calls. I know the sight of hawks circling around a distant road looking for roadkill, which distant rainclouds will soon burst, the subtle changes in vegetation on Country.'

'I trust you,' I say, releasing my fists to motion to him with my hands. 'It's just the other rescuers don't know that Dreaming here and nobody knows which way we went from that ranger hut.'

I feel shame admitting my lack of knowledge and I know it's my own fault that I've forgotten what he taught me out bush when I was younger. I'd chosen playing footy or hanging out with mates in town over trips out with the old man. He hadn't really been out that much lately either, to be honest though. When I did head out it was with family for a barbeque around a waterhole, fishing with my mates, hunting just out of town for turkey with my uncles. I hadn't been interested in going out with any of the Elders really and when they were there I hadn't wanted to sit and listen to them yarning about the old times or Creation. My aunties had pointed out how lucky we were to still even have that connection; they'd said some groups had lost it through invasion, colonisation, Stolen Generation and all the policies that went with it. Those aunties said that some mob weren't even allowed to talk language or share Creation stories; some had been taken far from their Country never to return.

'I've been picking my landmarks as I walk,' I say quietly. We always do it; it's like second nature. You choose landmarks so that you always know where you are headed and where you have come from.

'You know this Country, in your heart,' Grandfather says, stopping by a large tree and carving an 'X' on it with a knife. 'And we'll do this whitefella way of making marks so that our mate Officer Thomas can find us,' Grandfather laughs at me, 'plus you've got that fancy old map.'

I hate that I'd shown weakness. I can hear Grandfather's heavy breathing as he matches my steady pace. He is gently singing one of the songlines in language. It feels familiar, connecting me to the Country, to Creation.

In the distance, we hear a loud wail. I gulp down the fear that jumps to my throat. And again I'm on edge.

'What bush sound is that?' I ask my grandfather as he walks up beside me. He cocks his head, listening.

'I'm not sure,' Grandfather admits slowly, thinking back through his previous experiences. 'It almost sounds familiar.'

The wail continues. The strange feeling in my throat grows tighter.

'It sounds like it is getting louder!' I whisper hoarsely, the words struggling to escape my mouth.

8
MURDERERS, MONSTERS AND MANIA

To my horror, Grandfather begins walking towards the sound.

'What are you doing?' I whisper urgently, trying to grab Grandfather's hand. 'We have to go back! Get help.'

'It could be something to do with your cousin,' Grandfather replies calmly. His breathing is deep and slow, considered, brave and strong. I feel ashamed of my fast-beating heart and the fact that I have lied about the second person I am out here to find. The fact that I have not told my grandfather about my fears with the tyre prank.

'Let's get the police!' I whisper urgently. I want to help them and back home in the town I'd run as fast as anyone to help a Countryman but Grandfather's talk of supernatural has got to me. Plus, the fact that the police aren't sure if there is a murderer hiding out here has added to the lump growing in my stomach. We need backup here. An old man and a teenager are no match for a killer ... or a monster. 'We can't help anyone if we are dead!'

'We can sneak up on kangaroos in the bush, you've got stealth,' Grandfather responds. 'We'll just see what it is. Bush sounds, your schoolmates, the murderer or a monster. Either way, the police aren't here and that noise sounds urgent.'

Monsters? As Grandfather mentions monsters again my mind fills with the images from the stories he told me as a child. My imagination is good. The images cruelly distorted, dark. I can't think. Adrenaline surges through my body. Conflicted, I want to run in the opposite direction. Grandfather's talk of monsters is starting to get to me. And that scream sounds close enough to be in my skull.

I picture a monster of Grandfather's Dreaming biting into Jenny's soft neck ... the same neck I kissed that one night at the party. The neck I am forbidden from kissing like I did by Law. I find my courage again. We need to do something.

I tug off my backpack and reach into the survival kit. My hand finds the UHF radio.

'Officer Thomas? Do you copy?' I yell into the handset but there's only a loud crackle on the other end.

I am angry. At myself for not remembering to radio for backup earlier and at him for not coming back to help yet. He is probably walking around clueless back at the camp site or, even worse, has given up looking for two blokes gone walkabout and headed to the main camp site on the main track into the park. Or just headed back to the crash site and dumped us out here.

'Mayday, mayday!' I repeat into the radio. 'I think someone is hurt ... we can hear crying out ...' Or monster, I think to myself, letting go of the speaker button.

Still nothing. The thick bush and hills must be blocking out the signal. We'll need to find higher ground.

'Be quiet,' Grandfather commands.

I realise the screaming has stopped. The forest is quiet, other than the loud crackle of the radio. I switch it off. Fear builds in the pit of my stomach. I had been loud. Had I alerted the fugitive murderer?

Did Grandfather's monster hear us? Even my breathing sounds loud as I wait to find out.

Grandfather stoops low and drags me down with him.

We creep through the undergrowth making as little noise as possible. Thudump, thump, thump; my heart beats loudly in my ears and vibrates out through the forest, muffling my hearing. I notice with horror that Grandfather has somehow unhooked his hunting knife from its pocket in his pack. I try to control my breathing. I wish I had brought a hunting knife too. Instead I grab a thick stick from the ground and grip it in my hands. This has all got pretty serious pretty quick.

It is eerily silent. All the birdlife has been scared away by the racket. The insects are silent. My palms are sweaty. I follow Grandfather forward, shallow breathing.

The trees begin to thin out. I realise with relief that we are on an open dirt track.

'An old firebreak that must run through the park,' Grandfather whispers, more to himself than to me. 'That makes sense.'

It doesn't make any sense to me.

'They might have had to travel the back road into the park if that fire was over the road. Maybe they never reached either camp site. That's why there was not any sign of them there.'

I bend down, instantly finding the bus tracks in the soft dirt.

'Why would they ...'

The trees at the edge of the dirt track rattle. There's another blood-curdling wail.

I freeze. Grandfather stays still, moving only his eyes, scanning the tree line; his hand grips the hunting knife. Twigs crack. My heart beats loudly.

9
CONNECTION

There's a hiss from the bushes. Feathers flap. I move forward, taking care with each footfall not to make a sound. The fact that the owner of the hiss doesn't know we are here is the only advantage we have.

I realise now I can't be second-guessing myself. We are here. They are out there. We can't let them face whatever it is alone. No matter how out of my depth I feel, I'd never forgive myself if anyone got hurt. I put my finger to my lips and crouch down low. I slowly, silently spread the lowest branches of the shrub, making sure they do not even rustle with the movement. I peer in.

A pair of curlew birds are taking turns to jump towards the trunk of a tree. The curlew bird lets out a scream and pecks again, attempting to catch a cicada off the tree. The insect shrieks too. Together their cries make the wail I had thought was a monster. I feel anger surge through my body, annoyed that I had listened to the fairy stories of the old man, ashamed that I had been afraid.

'The devil bird,' Grandfather sighs, body relaxing. I almost laugh as my anger subsides to relief, although we still haven't found the camp.

I know about the devil bird. An ironic name right now. We have been warned about the devil bird since we were little. The old people say they trick babies and young children into the bush with their screams. A tale to stop young children running off into the bush alone. It had kind of worked this time on us. It is not one of Grandfather's imaginary Creation creatures at all, and it's not a mass-student-murdering criminal.

I walk back to the dirt track, my grandfather trailing behind. I bend to look at the tyre tracks again. He studies the depth of the marks on each side. Grandfather squats down next to me and I take a moment to breathe deeply and steady my heart rate. 'This way,' he announces.

We walk along the track for what feels like a long time. The hot sun beats down on my face sending a trail of sweat dripping from my nose. I wipe it off and wish for a breeze. Too much time to think. Jenny and Brook know Country well enough. Both of them would have come out this way when they were little with family too. Why had they come out this way this time?

I look back at my grandfather; he has dropped further behind. He needs to rest and so do I. I don't want to stop tracking but my head spins and my body feels weak. I need food.

'Let's stop,' I say as I wait for him to catch up. 'I'm starving.'

Grandfather gives me a disapproving look but I can tell he needs to rest too. I point to a tree trunk in the shade by the road; I motion that we should sit. I dig deep into my bag to find the snacks that Mum has packed.

'It is getting late,' Grandfather points to the sun getting lower in the sky. 'You need to eat quickly. We don't have much time especially if we are trying to get you back before dark.'

I know that more sharply than he could know. The game tonight is the only reason I didn't ride out here the second I heard the news, looking for Jenny and Brook. This kind of opportunity is once in a lifetime. But I am ashamed I'd even thought to put my aspirations before the lives of the mob in the bus. Ashamed even more since it could be my fault.

Now, though part of me feels like we are out on a wild-goose chase, a deeper part of me tells me we aren't. We don't even know if they have been found by someone else. I hope that Officer Thomas would call us with the news – if he could even get reception. I wonder if Grandfather would get a sense when they are found like he has one about them being lost?

Looking at my grandfather's muscled but frail body, hunched over his sandwich, I know it is important that I am here with him. I'm angry that my uncles left him behind. Even though he is not as strong or fast as he was as a young man, my grandfather had set the pace and I had been the one keeping up for most of the morning until now. Maybe my uncles asked him to stay at home and he organised Officer Thomas without letting family know. Surely, my family wouldn't leave him to go out bush himself and find his own way. I know better than to ask the old man. He is too proud to talk about his failing sight and slower body, let alone the disrespect my uncles would have shown if they did ignore him.

'Tell me about this teacher we are looking for,' Grandfather says as we scoff down our peanut butter and banana sandwiches. 'What do you know about the other year twelves?'

I think hard about them. Our family is related to most of the blakfellas in town, one way or another, so that was an easy place to start.

'Not much,' I remind Grandfather. 'Our mob for a start.'

Grandfather nods, pain and worry cross his face.

'Brooklyn is related to us,' Grandfather adds to the obvious information we both know. 'And Jenny has family from out our way.'

'Yep. I don't think they had anything to do with this,' I say thinking about my relatives. 'Brooklyn's too busy chasing her boyfriend around. That Asian fella in her grade, you know? Jenny's one of the good ones.'

There is nothing average about her though. She is amazing. Kind, funny, deadly at sport and smart. Great dancer, even better kisser ... Not that I want to share any of that with my grandfather.

'Yeah, I agree,' Grandfather says thoughtfully, connecting the information. 'Any trouble brewing in between anyone ... or anyone out at the station?'

I wonder how much my grandfather knows. How much he'd picked up from gossip after Michael's brother's death or how much he knew instinct way. Just thinking of Old Henry sends cold shivers down my spine. Maybe drowning was poetic justice.

I flick through the year 12s' faces in my mind, trying to piece together the snippets of time in town schooling with them here. I don't know them all well. Some groups in town just don't mix. Grandad knew as well as anyone about the divide in the town. He grew up when blakfellas weren't even allowed in the pub without a white person accompanying them. He told us stories of when they used to have to hide his light-skinned sister in shallow holes under the spinifex to keep her from being taken away by the police. Over time he'd even shared some of the ways the police used to target blakfellas for any crime in town and even beat a few real bad when they didn't admit to something they'd been pinned for.

For us now, we just dealt with the leftover feeling passed down from grandparents on both sides of town. Nobody really liked to call each other racist or prejudiced, but there was definitely a divide between the farming families and the Aboriginal mob, the rich kids and the farming kids, the immigrants and the rest of town. Our History teacher one year had tried to teach us about intergenerational trauma – something about the pain of your Elders getting passed down to you. I kind of saw what she meant, families who were broken apart and torn from land back in the day, didn't know how to deal with life in the new world. They'd seen their Country trampled by cattle, their family raped or massacred, their children stolen. They'd lived as second-class citizens without rights, their work unvalued or unpaid. That kind of stuff beats a person down. Some adults never grew up with their families but only in institutions so they didn't know how to bring up their kids. Some people had so much anger that they turned to drink to dull the pain. All that stuff is witnessed by kids younger than me and they feel the trauma as raw as if it happened to them too. It made me have hope the day Kevin Rudd said sorry. Like a weight lifted off my shoulders to watch my granny cry and let go of some of that pain. Then the racist stuff started on social media and I knew that sorry was only the start of the journey. I'd stolen a car that night. I needed to be away from the world that could say such yucky things. I'd returned it later, after the bitter taste of racism had been blown out the window at 120 down the highway.

That's why I kind of liked football. The same way. Wind in my hair sprinting down the green, ball bouncing in front of me. I can let all that go, you know, just focus on the moment. Out on the footy field we were all just the same.

'There's always some drama, Grandfather,' I half smile. 'It's high school.'

I think harder about anyone's connections to the station. I don't know a lot about all that, being from out on community – only the secondhand gossip I get from the boys. I find it really hard to believe that any of the 12s have any connection to that at all. They certainly couldn't have been involved with last night, but it gets me thinking about any motive a murderer, if it is even a murder, would have chasing any of the 12s out bush. If we do run into any murdering fugitive it's likely to be an accident while they hide out bush ... and the likelihood of that is almost non-existent in the millions of acres of red-dirt bushland. Thinking it through helps me feel calmer about one of the scenarios that had been playing on repeat in my head. Now I just had to worry about stranded and injured schoolmates ... and Grandfather's superstitions.

'You know how old Mr Henry was selling sly grog out to the dry communities? Some of the under-age kids in town also go out there to get sly grog if they can't get it in town. I know Rocky and Jefferey's gang sometimes get their alcohol that way. Their parents are too strict to let them drink and they can't be seen getting anyone to buy it for them from the bottlos; their families would kill them. Not any reason for any of them to be caught up in something more suspicious though I don't think.'

I leave out my involvement. That I'd been there too. How Henry had dealt in more than black market liquor. How his drugs had led to Michael's brother's death. For a second I contemplate the possibility that someone might have bought some drugs or grog on camp. I picture them face down floating in the water like Michael's brother had been.

'Any pranksters in that class?' Grandfather probes, eyes scrunched, watching me carefully as I answer. Perhaps he knows I am not telling him the whole truth.

'Jefferey, Scotty, Rocky and Caleb I'd say,' I reply, glad of the questions as they move me away from the dark images that were floating through my mind. I remember overhearing Jefferey and Scotty planning their upcoming graduation stunt. In this moment, I really hope we find them because if anyone was going to pull off putting all the classroom furniture on the roof of the school, it was those clowns.

Jefferey is short and stocky and he already helps

his dad at the local mechanics shop. As well as fixing local vehicles and busted-up tourist cars, his dad gets the big mechanic parts for the stations and mines. He is a bit of a bully, not afraid to throw his weight around on the footy field either. There was a rumour a while back that Jefferey's dad might be working with someone on the stations getting hard drugs up to sell around town. Although if we believed all the small town rumours then there'd be twenty bad things true about me. Not all of them would be wrong. I wish it had just been a rumour and I could just brush it away. Not the cold truth. I'd seen the evidence.

Rocky is another townie from my family's end of town. His father works early morning shifts at the bakery. I was in town schooling when I was in year 7, can't remember exactly what for, maybe my mum was giving birth to one of my little brothers, anyway Rocky and his mates put flour up on the office doors and classroom fans. It was hilarious watching the principal storm around the school, searching for the culprits and looking like a ghost in flour ... until someone turned on the fan in our room and we all ran out coughing and laughing. Rocky hadn't really thought through the prank enough though ... they should have put it on their room fans too because it really narrowed down the search given there were only thirty flour-free students laughing at the rest of us.

'I just don't see why they would pull a prank out here. And even if they did, I can't think how they'd get stuck out here because of it,' I sigh, thinking hard. The food has helped me focus.

'Any of them capable of doing something stupid that would put them all in danger?' Grandfather prompts.

'One of the year twelves is definitely a bully; I know a lot of kids in my year he's beaten up,' I reply, thinking about all the school rumours that might give Grandfather the clue he is searching for. 'Maybe he hurt someone and they got stuck waiting for help? Or maybe Hannah ... you know the girl that was involved in the hit and run? You remember, she was in the news and she got let off for good behaviour ... or maybe her expensive lawyers did a good job!'

'I know her. There were rumours when she was born that her mum had an affair with a blakfella from community. That mum was quickly married up to the Stockman farming family, if I remember rightly? Big money family,' Grandfather reflects.

'Come on, Grandfather,' I say, pulling myself up and wiping the red dirt off my shorts. I offer a hand down to my grandfather. 'We can talk and walk.'

I feel bad for rushing him as he grunts with the effort of pulling himself up. We both know what could be at stake.

'Rumour was she was off her face on drugs or alcohol,' I add to Grandfather's memory. 'They didn't think to test a pretty, rich, white girl.'

'We don't know all the details, Dek. She was under-age, they might not have even thought about that or were waiting for her parents? Maybe those type of drug tests weren't up here at the time,' my grandfather defends the police. 'We'd be no better than that woman jumping to assumptions back at the cliff. Most of the police mob out here are good, hardworking people.'

'Well it smelt dirty to me,' I spit. The thought of corruption and racism again bringing the bitter taste in my mouth. I change the subject, 'Do you think they have the helicopters out looking yet?'

I want this over. I want to find Brooklyn and Jenny. I want to look over her body to make sure she is unhurt, to feel her arms around me ... There is just enough time to get back to town in time for the match.

'They'll have a tough time seeing anything out here,' Grandfather says, worry in his voice. 'There are some patches of pretty thick bush around the rivers and waterholes, a few big hills too. Even in the sparse scrub it'll be tough to spot anything from above. If that bus has been covered in red dust or they parked under a tree to get shade, those spotters will have a hard time seeing anything. Not to mention, this national park is a big area to cover. And looking near the campgrounds won't necessarily get them near here anytime soon.'

That doesn't fill me with confidence. After all, we are alone, in the very bushland that Grandfather is talking about. Grandfather brushes the loose twigs from his legs.

'See that rock face over there in the distance?' Grandfather asks, as though reading my mind. We continue walking at a steady pace as he points around. 'That's connected to the Creation songlines ... we can follow that ridge to a deep, cool waterhole that is safe for drinking all year round. We are not lost, my grandson.'

The hot sun beats down on my head and back. Usually around this time, out bush for any other reason, we'd be lounging around in the shade of the big trees or floating around in a sheltered waterhole. It's not like I haven't run around in the dry desert heat before though. Sometimes when I was younger I would help my uncles out mustering on a station. I know the risk of dehydration out here and take another swig of my water bottle. There are stories of tourists being found dead out bush with water still in their bottle. You're not meant to ration it; you're meant to keep hydrated for as long as you can.

As we walk, the rough track takes us by a hill with crumbling sides. Rocks, eroded a long time past, litter the base of the hill. A long, deep shelf has been carved by the elements in one section. Not deep enough to really be called a cave but the shelf of rock creates a cool sanctuary beneath it. I look at the tyre tracks and wish again that we were in a troopy instead of trekking on foot through the bush. Some sections of the road are that eroded that it would have been slow work even with a vehicle. There must have been some rain out this way, unlike in community where we were still waiting for the dry to break. The long lead-up to the wet is always hot and dry – we all wait with anticipation and when the first rains come kids run from classrooms to dance and jump in the big, warm raindrops.

A flash of white catches my eye. I quickly turn my head, eyes squinted against the sharp light, steps faltering. My grandfather senses my change in pace and stops to watch and listen too. I motion him to stay quiet with a flick of my hand. My eyes rest on some ochre smudged onto the outer rock near the ledge of the shelf.

'Thought I saw something out of the corner of my eye,' I say aloud, realising that my heightened state had drawn my attention to the stark white contrast. I squish up my lips and pout them over in the direction, as us mob do instead of point. 'Just over there.'

Grandfather looks in the direction I have indicated and walks over. I follow, enjoying the relief from the sun as we pass into the shade. It feels cool and still under the ledge. Grandfather places his hand against the cool rock. I notice that there are splatters of ochre paint all over the rock face. My family had taken me out to look at rock art before, special places to our people that even tourists didn't usually go. My grandfather had said it was important to keep some places secret because when the white man came they would chip off rock art to send back as souvenirs or off to museums. When the land rights movement started, station workers would smash up rock to hide evidence of our history on the land. Sometimes in the early days, even our ancestors' bones would be sent off to museums, sometimes without proper identification, to be locked in random storerooms and lost.

I'm drawn to a figure high up on the wall. Small, faded. It's hard to make out. I want to touch it, to feel the connection. Moving my hand up towards it a shiver shoots down my spine and I withdraw quickly. Shocked I walk out into the sun. I try to explain it away to myself as just a cramp or pins and needles or something else everyday, normal. I want to ask my grandfather more about it but something holds me back. I'm almost apprehensive to hear the answer. A question for another time I realise as I look up at the sinking sun. My heart sinks at the realisation that there probably won't be time now even if we were to find the 12s, to get radio contact and be lucky enough to be airlifted. That reminds me that I haven't tried to get radio contact for a while and I pull out the UHF from my pack. No reply.

'We might get better reception up the hill,' Grandfather says. I look at the beads of sweat captured in his bushy white brows.

'I'll go, Grandfather,' I say, pointing back to the rock outcrop. 'Get a bit of rest in the shade? I'll be back in a second.'

I'm used to climbing the crumbling red hills around our community so I spread my centre of gravity and climb quickly. I can hear the tinkle of the small rocks falling down the hill behind me. My breath quickens, the hot air giving no relief with each inward motion. I stop a few metres up the side; looking out across the landscape I try to radio again. I will myself to see the flash of reflection from the bus windscreen, or a splash of colour from a school uniform or the smoke of a cooking fire. The landscape remains red, dusty and barren spotted with thick areas of trees and bush only broken by rounded hills.

'Officer Thomas? Do you read?' the crackle of the radio remains static. 'This is Deklan Archer. Does anybody read?' I try again hoping to catch someone out this way gold detecting or hiking. Anyone to relay our location so they can come pick us up to continue the trip by car. Aircon. Rest my sore leg. I'd forgotten about the pain. The heat took precedence. Now I'm reminded, I feel like the dull throbbing starts on cue.

The crackle on the radio changes but I can't hear anything properly. I quickly climb to the top of the hill. No luck there and nothing more to see. From all directions it is the same landscape.

I scramble down. Grandfather studies my face as I reach the bottom. In silent agreement we keep walking fast along the dirt track. There is no need for tracking now so we are keeping a better pace. In some parts the trees have grown low over the road, forcing us to weave around them, while the bus we are looking for would have just pushed its way through. In other parts we walk along the deep ridges left by eroding streams of rain. It must have been fairly recent; there were shallow puddles in the deeper dips. On others the track is full of light red sand that our feet sink deep into.

I let my mind drift back to my football disappointment, keeping my senses alert. I feel guilty that I am even worrying about the football match that will be starting soon. Finding my schoolmates, my family, Jenny is a priority. Finding out that I am not responsible for them being missing and that they are all just fine taking an extra day to relax by a waterhole, unaware of all the drama. In my dreams. Then again, maybe they have already been found, safe and sound, and now they are out looking for the silly old man and teen who went looking for them. I wonder if anyone will at least mention my name to the recruiters. Maybe coach will show some footage of our training matches.

Maybe I'll still have a shot. I know some boys from up our way that travelled away to boarding school in Perth or Melbourne or Adelaide and got recruited in the drafts. I can't imagine going to one of those fancy schools though. Putting up with pushy teachers and rich kids. They'd never pick me anyway. Bush kid, little juvie record, okay grades at school. This recruiting thing could have been my one big chance to make something of myself. Finding the bus and everyone well will show I'm not a murderer at least, I guess.

A white bird flies startled from a tree as we push through an overgrown section of the road. The flash of colour reminds me of the painting back at the ledge. Had I imagined the feeling? What had the marking been? It had kind of looked like a human figure although so faded it was hard to tell.

The night is falling quickly and the dirt track continues to weave its way through the national park. Occasionally we lose sight of the track covered with dirt, or over patches of hard rock, but there is no sign that the bus went off road into the bush so we continue to follow the path. I keep trying the radio. I'm annoyed that we haven't spotted any helicopters out looking for us ... or them ... or whatever else might be out here with us.

I am relieved when we finally reach the edge of the ridge. My legs hurt. My back hurts from carrying the pack. I look over at my grandfather trailing slightly behind. His eyes are down, focusing on each step in front of him, breathing heavy. I can only imagine what the families back home are thinking. I feel bad that I am now pushing us forward.

'This way,' Grandfather pants, pointing with his lips towards a steep gully. Inside it opens up into the waterhole sheltered at its base. I can make out some features of the steep red hill. The vegetation is thick and green, flourishing near the constant water source.

I feel defeated. 'Shouldn't we keep looking?'

'I can scout out around our camp while you rest. It's too dangerous for you to track them at night though. We don't know what we are up against,' Grandfather sounds flat too. I want to argue back, but looking at his old, thin body as he leans against the cool rock wall I can see that this rest is as much for him as it is for me.

The last rays of dusk light slowly creep behind the hills.

I've always loved waiting for dusk to go hunting for kangaroo with my family. Some of the station owners use them for target practice. One thing my mother made sure I learnt: we only kill to eat. It kind of disgusted me watching my uncle's station worker mates take aim at kangaroos, not that I could say anything without them taking the piss or laying in to me, the young fella tagging along. It kind of seems a bit rough to me that the roos were there first, you know, minding their own business. Just because station owners claimed the land to run cattle and grow a few crops, the roos have to get off the Country too or be used like that.

It kind of reminds me of how the station owners invaded our Country to run their cattle, dirtying the waterholes, trampling Sacred ground – that they massacred and poisoned our people to get us off the Country too. It always bugged me a bit when I went out to help my cousins and uncles running stations. Some of the station owners in the early days had massacred our mob; they had used us as slave labour paying in food items or even as bad as the Government 'holding' people's pay and then never actually paying them. It kind of just feels wrong sometimes to be mustering cattle on the same stations that all that history happened on. Some of those stations are still owned by the same family lines, some by big international conglomerates making money off our sweat but a few are First Nations owned now too. Same time my mob are some of the best jackaroos and jillaroos in the whole damn country. Some of them mob know the land like they know the back of their hands.

Watching the news one time I saw what happens to some of our cattle in the other countries that they get shipped to. It kind of made me ashamed. Us mob go out to get a 'killer', what we call fresh beef, and stuff but most of us are respectful. We shoot to kill and use it all for something. I can imagine being shipped off, stinking hot all squished up together. It must be like what our mob back in the day felt like when they were chained by the neck walking through desert or when they would ship us off to prison islands or missions during Stolen Generation time.

Mum used to be good like that though. She never teased me for thinking outside the box, questioning things, seeing things from a different perspective. She reminded me how we are connected to the land and all the animals on it through our Creation. I was reminded that we must show respect to our animal brothers.

But as night falls tonight I feel completely different. It kind of feels like we are the hunted.

10

THE PACK

Something just doesn't feel right. I can't place it. That niggly feeling I had had all day since finding out the news. The back of my neck tingles, like we are being watched.

'You set up the camp and I'll have a look around for some tucker.' My grandfather has put down his pack under a tree. 'We better save that dried stuff for when we reach the rest of them.'

'Don't go too far, old man,' I say jokingly with a wink. My grandfather raises his eyebrows at me, then nods his head. It's not the time for jokes.

As he walks around the camp site, experienced eyes carefully looking for bush food, I start getting out our supplies and setting up a small cooking fire. We are good at the camping routine even though it feels like ages since I have been camping with the old man. When I used to go out camping with the family us kids would collect the wood for the fire and dig the soaks. Our old people would teach us how to find bushtucker plants and how to catch our food. I'm glad Grandfather's finding some tucker: nothing beats fresh even if the small collection of dried stuff in our bags would be easier. I hope he is right that that mob will be hungry for the dried food ... that would mean they are alive.

Grandfather has walked out of sight now but I can hear him just beyond the rock and trees. My eyes dart around the small clearing we have. Two sides of the clearing are blocked by large red rock walls, leaving only two directions that we could be snuck up on. The waterhole fills most of the remaining space between the two sides. The other side appears to be similar thick trees like this side. You got to be careful in places like this for flash flooding. It helps to calm my nerves knowing that there isn't really a chance for anything to sneak up on us ... and yet if they did ... we'd be trapped.

I dig a shallow hole and move the undergrowth away leaving a clear circle. I put the small twigs and dry grass at the bottom and build up the larger sticks leaning over it. In the old days we would have lit the fire with flint, or carried embers in a round clay or carved coolamon. Today, I flick the lighter and gently blow. Before Europeans invaded, my mob used to use fire to manage the land, clear it and encourage fresh growth. In school in year 6, they tried to teach us that Aboriginal tribes used to be nomadic and lived as hunter-gatherers, by chance, but my Elders told a different story. I'd been happy when I found a book called *Dark Emu* in the school library that proved my teacher wrong. She hadn't been so happy to be pulled up by a little cheeky student like me though. She'd kept me in to tell me off about answering back and talking over the teacher.

By the time the fire has sparked Grandfather has returned with a feed of goanna. We gut him and place him on the hot coals with some branches on top to help keep the heat in.

My mouth waters in anticipation of the first bite. Goanna is one of my favourite foods: juicy and rich, kind of like chicken. It makes me proud that we can get a feed off Country any time. Our Country provides. It makes more sense to me to get fresh bushtucker anytime than to eat that plastic-wrapped meat. You don't know how long it's been sitting there or how it was slaughtered or even where it was from. A teacher showed us something about animal rights in English one year and it kind of made sense to me. It doesn't really seem right to breed up animals in small cages and then drag them kicking and crying out to get their throats slit in front of the rest of them. At least our way we know we kill them right. Ours is part of our culture. The other way ... just kind of feels cruel. I'll eat meat from the shop occasionally but it's Aboriginal way to share a catch with your family so we always have fresh barra or beef or turkey or goanna or something coming in.

Grandfather hands me a leg. I eat it off the bone. Fat dripping out as I bite into the juicy flesh.

We sit quietly staring into the embers both deep in our own thoughts. My mind flickers back and forth like the tiny flames. I wonder if any of my friends were picked to represent at the state competition. Did Willum get back to play in time? A pinch of jealousy settles in my gut. The likelihood of those recruiter mob coming up this way again might be pretty slim. My family don't have money to send me down that way to try out for the development squads and I wouldn't fit in at any of those fancy boarding schools. Then my thoughts shift to Ms Pritchard and the students on camp. Were they just stranded somewhere but safe? Ms Pritchard had Brook and Jenny with her who would know how to find bushtucker and dig a soak if they found a water source. They just had to wait it out to be found. Then again maybe they already had been. Surely that cop or our family would be out following Grandfather's marks and our tracks by now if the school mob had been found. A shiver shoots down my spine at the other alternatives. They are all dead from dehydration or a bus crash ... because of me. Maybe they were in the wrong spot at the wrong time in the path of a fleeing murderer who hijacked the bus and mass murdered them all. Worse still, maybe our ancestors didn't like that teacher dragging all them white kids out this deep and those Creation beings found them.

Grandfather nudges my knee with a stick, pointing to the honeycombed hills around us, lit by the flickering firelight, 'I ever tell you the story of this place?'

I shake my head. He tells me in our language. I am good at understanding traditional language. It's the speaking that me and the rest of my cousins sometimes get stuck with. We can all code switch back and forth between English and Kriol and our language.

Choosing the best words to get our idea across. Cause we live in community we don't have to talk English lots though, just to teachers mostly. But I can't speak fluently in language either. Us kids understand a few different languages from the groups in our area but no one our age really just talks in their language all the time. Something I should try to do more of maybe. Listening to Grandfather's story reminds me that he won't be around forever to tell it this way. This story takes me back in time. I can picture my grandfather sitting by his grandfather under different circumstances in a different time. These hills feel eternal and so does the story.

He shifts uncomfortably, stretching out his old legs, 'Sleep time.'

It's humid even at night in the build-up to the wet so we just unroll the light blankets that my mother had packed and lie out under the stars. Lying down I finally have time to feel the exhaustion in my body. My legs feel like they could melt into the red desert ground. The dull ache in my leg continues and feels more intense than earlier now that my whole focus is on my body. Still, I sleep.

My eyes flutter open unsure if it was a dream or something in real life that has awoken me. The clear night sky is alight with the shine of a billion stars. I put my arms behind my head and gaze. I can spot the constellations my Elders have taught me. A twig cracks. My heart beat jumps. I listen. Slowly I turn my head to look around. The contents of our bags lays sprawled out around our camp site. Had I been that exhausted that I had slept through the noise it must have inevitably caused? My eyes fall to my grandfather's blanket: empty. My mind races. Normally, this wouldn't be alarming. Here, now, it is.

I move one hand to my side, then the next. Pushing my torso up one vertebrae at a time. Eyes flicking around the dark shadows, ears alert to every rustle, crack and whisper. I bend one knee, then the next and push myself into squatting position, planning my next move. I reach for a stick just within my grasp and bring it protectively to my chest.

I crouch low and move forward towards the way we had entered the valley, towards the sound. Steadying myself to startle my grandfather mid piss, and readying myself to find the more gruesome scene my imagination is dreaming up.

I notice a ripped map, the lighter and some other items scattered to the dark as I move. I urge my eyes to readjust to the dark as I move deeper into the undergrowth. A dark figure is crouched closer to the rock wall, back to me. I raise my stick. The figure flicks its head in my direction. The whites of its eyes flash. At the sight of Grandfather's white beard I let out an audible sigh and am about to talk when he holds his finger to his lips. He points to the ground. I look towards my feet and scan. Scattered prints, although I can't make them out in this low light. I hear more rustling ahead. Am I moving towards a Creation being?

Slightly closer I make them out. Feral dogs or maybe dingos feasting on something in one of our packs. I count four.

'Go, get you mongrels,' I shout automatically, used to scaring off the camp dogs back home from our yard. My grandfather shakes his head in annoyance at my outburst and quickly withdraws his knife from his pants.

The wild dogs look up and growl. I should have been more cautious; wild dogs aren't like the cheeky dogs back home. These dogs haven't learnt to fear man yet. One dog crouches forward on its limbs, a deep warning growl escaping through bared teeth. I'm sure my grandfather and I can ward off these mongrels with my heavy stick and his knife but I'm not sure it would be injury free and out here that could be deadly. Do we back down?

I catch his eye and flick my head towards the trees, 'Go!' The pack leader leaps forward with its pack mates close behind. Grandfather moves first, fast for an old man. Adrenaline does that when it's fight or flight – life or death. I race towards the closest tall tree and climb. Jumping, my hands grab a large branch, my legs searching for a grip on the trunk, sending shooting pain down my legs at the sudden exertion. I'm up just in time as two of the dogs reach me, jumping and barking at the base. Their teeth sparkle in the low moonlight. Breathing heavily I look back towards my grandfather. He's made it into a tree in the middle of the valley while I am closer to the rock face. It's thinner than my tree and bends dangerously under his weight. I have to get the dogs away from him.

'Argh, get off!' I growl, kicking out with my feet. 'Get away!'

I grab at the branches and snap off the ones I can, throwing them towards the dogs at the base of my grandfather's tree. The pack run between the two trees barking, jumping and biting. Grandfather can't risk moving in case he shakes the tree. I look around desperately and notice that I am almost within arm's reach of the rock wall. Edging out onto the branch further I am just able to grab a handful of rocks and begin throwing them towards the dogs. I hit one on the side of the head, sending it whimpering back towards the bag. I throw again and hit the dog nipping at my grandfather's feet. It strikes it on the hind leg, the strong muscle absorbing some of the pain; it turns around towards me growling. I throw again, hitting it on the muzzle. It yelps and backs up, as if judging its chances, and then runs.

We wait, ears straining to hear where they have gone in the dark. Grandfather jumps down from his tree with a thud. I climb down quickly to join him.

'Are you okay?' I ask, scanning his body and supporting him up.

'I'm fine,' he replies, voice tight. 'Bloody mongrels shredded your bag through.'

We move towards where the wild dogs had been feasting. A scattering of rubbish remains. The pack itself is nowhere to be seen. My shoulders slump. I drop to the ground searching though the remaining items. Another map, some ripped packets of food. No UHF. A new type of fear grips my body. Not that the UHF had proven all that useful so far but it was our lifeline to the outside world.

I collect up the other items again in silence and follow Grandfather back to our camp site. I know our camp fire will keep the wild dogs away; I shouldn't have let it die down. I stuff the remaining items into the old man's bag and lie down on my blanket. I feel responsible for him and lie awake, alert, listening. As the adrenaline leaves my body I'm just left numb. I sleep. I dream of monsters.

11
GUILT

I wake up with a sore back, disorientated. It takes a couple of seconds for the realisation of where I am to settle in ... and then the memory of why. I quickly look around for my grandfather and see him still asleep in the low morning light. He looks frail and old. I am reluctant to wake him so I set about putting water and dirt on the fire that is still burning strongly.

'Grandfather,' I gently shake him awake, 'we should get going.'

He too wakes up dazed and as the veil of dreams slips from his eyes, he says urgently, 'We are close, and there is great danger. I can feel it.'

I shiver. I know he is right.

'We lost the UHF,' I whisper, I hold out my hand to help him up.

'Us mob have been signalling each other long before those contraptions, my boy,' Grandfather grunts as he rolls up his sleeping gear. I grab it off him and stuff it in the remaining pack. I walk over to check for any last cooking things that might be on the ground.

Grandfather bends down to put the pack on his back. I rush over and grab it instead. A younger grandfather would have pushed me off and ruffled my hair. I can see that this trip is taking its toll. He stoops to fill up our water bottles with the fresh, clean water from a soak he has dug by the edge of the waterhole and motions that we should leave.

We finally rejoin the fire track. The tyre marks are easy to spot. Grandfather sets a quick pace. It makes me more nervous. It's the coolest part of the day and I am thankful for the slight breeze that brushes my sweaty face.

After what feels like too long Grandfather stops. He bends down and picks up something black from the ground.

'Rubber from a tyre. Looks like it was punctured,' Grandfather declares, gathering his breath. My heart sinks. 'Look at how the tyre track changes from here. We must be close.'

He hands me the piece of tyre. A small, jagged piece of metal still stuck in it.

A punctured tyre out bush isn't that uncommon. Neither is old scraps of metal. It could be anyone's tyre. But inside I know it isn't.

I point up ahead to where the red dirt road rounds a bend already breaking into a run.

'They can't have limped much further up here,' I shout back to him.

'Stay close, who knows what shape they'll all be in after a few days in the bush,' Grandfather calls out behind me.

I look back at the old man following with an urgent pace. I can't stop. I can hardly breathe. As I reach the bend, I hold my breath, afraid of what I might see.

The orange, four-wheel drive bus is on its side; the shredded tyre is blurred by the shadows of the nearby trees. I quickly scan the area remembering my first-aid training to look for 'danger', hoping not to see the bodies of the 12s but steeling myself for the worst. I reach the bus seconds before Grandfather. Feathers are scattered across the road. There are no tents to show the year 12s set up a camp. I pull myself up onto the bus and scramble to the bent door.

I pull hard on the bent door just as Grandfather catches up. It comes away with a loud crack. Heart racing I lower myself down.

The chairs creak violently under my added weight. Frustrated, I wait trying to see into the darkness. Shattered glass, belongings strewn around. No people. No dead bodies. Yet.

'No one in there,' I say as I climb back out, 'but it looks like lots of luggage was left behind.'

Grandfather grabs my hands to pull me up. Blood covers my skin.

12
GROUND ZERO

'Shit, you're bleeding!'

I rub my hands over my pants, 'Don't worry about me, we have to find them.' Grandfather pours the water over my bloodied hands and holds it out for me to take a sip from.

'It's not your blood,' Grandfather says, eyes watering as his voice breaks.

'There is a fair bit of blood in there,' I reply, thinking of the splatters on the smashed windows.

I try to process this piece of information. Does that mean the year 12s are injured or dead? Does that mean *I killed them*?

'So where are they?' I manage to stutter. In shock

the possibility of one of the Creation beings devouring them feels more real. 'We have to find them.'

'I didn't say they were dead,' Grandfather replies quietly, the reality of the situation clear in his sombre voice. 'But if they are out there injured they will be a lot easier to find.'

Why would they leave the bus? Why didn't they just follow the road back the way they had come? Or wait it out?

My knees feel weak. I'm not worthy of finding the group. There should be a whole police and rescue team helping. Why hadn't Officer Thomas caught up? I just want to go sink in the dirt. I just want to forget this day and pretend I had never mucked around with the tyres.

My uncles would probably just be arriving back out bush ready to look for the 12s again. The police should be coordinating today's air search. I wish they would hurry up and find us. This isn't the job of an old man ... and a murderer. Can't I take it all back? Reverse time. I want the safety of my room, the distraction of my phone, the warmth of some hot toast and tea. I can't wind back time, I'm here. We are all here because of me. More importantly, I want to be moving and finding them ... now.

My mind runs through a million courses of action and tries to figure out which one is the best right now. How do we get to them and get them help? I point back down into the bus, 'They'd have a UHF in there, right?'

Grandfather nods. He is sitting cross-legged on the side of the bus, face contorted, deep in thought. I'm going to have to get in there again. Carefully I lower myself into the bus, moving my feet around until they find leverage on the side of a bus seat. I monkey climb to the front dashboard and disconnect the UHF speaker from its cradle.

'Officer? Ranger? Anyone?' I radio. 'Mayday. Urgent backup requested!' When there is no response, I yell, 'Why aren't we getting anyone?'

'The hills around here. Obstructing the signal,' Grandfather replies with a frown. 'Hand me up that handset.'

'Bus located – approximately thirty ks northwest of old camp site on old fire access track. Tracking missing persons. Urgent police and ambulance requested. Copy?'

Silence.

Grandfather repeats his directions.

'Bus ... west of ... Copy?' the crackled reply comes through. My heart leaps, eyes open wide with relief.

Grandfather repeats his message again.

'... sending support ... await backup ... ETA ... hour ...' the reply comes.

'What does that mean?' I ask.

'At least the choppers will be closer to our location, even if they didn't get the whole message,' Grandfather sounds more confident than I have heard him all day.

'Check in the bag if the flares are still there,' I tell Grandfather, remembering some of the contents of the old emergency kit from the hut.

Grandfather tears the flare package and aims it high. He clicks the trigger. Nothing.

He hits it against the side of the bus and aims again. It splutters and misfires. A small fire burns at the gun mouth. Slipping off the bus, Grandfather grabs some grass off the ground and lights it in the middle of the dirt road.

'We can't let off a flare, but they will see the smoke of this fire,' he motions for me to grab twigs and leaves to build the fire up. He places lots of leaves and grass on top to make it smoke.

I'm glad he has placed it in the middle of the road. At the end of the dry season the bush is like tinder. The fire across the highway was evidence of the intensity these fires can burn at. A few years back now some marathon runners were brutally burnt in a scrub fire that the organisers had underestimated. You can never be too careful with fire in the bush. Especially when we don't know where the busload of teens are.

'Let's get going,' I say, spotting some blood on the track. Fear builds in my belly.

'From the look of that blood, it's been pooling for a while, maybe days,' Grandfather reasons. 'They might not have water, food or shelter ... and bleeding ... If the heat of the days and cold of the nights haven't weakened them then they'd need to watch out for wild dogs, snakes, spiders ... monsters. We don't have time to waste. I know this forest better than the police. You are right, let's go.'

My heart aches when I think of my cousins, when I think of Jenny's beautiful face covered in blood. I'm scared, my legs are shaking. But I'm determined. The knowledge that *I* caused this and now knowing clearly the danger makes me want to vomit.

Grandfather clasps my shoulder. 'I am glad you came. You are stronger than me these days both ways. You've made me proud.'

I nod. Unable to respond. Shame fills me up. I

take a deep breath and slowly pace around the bus searching for clues in the small details using my new knowledge from the past day plus my years of tracking animals in the bush. I duck down to touch a puddle of blood on the dirt. I motion into the bush.

'That way.'

'Why would they go into the bush?' Grandfather whispers as we start towards the tree line, shaking his head.

'To hide ...' There is a growing tightness in my stomach as we walk forward. As I say the words I wonder if I am right.

13
ACCIDENTS

At first there is a decent, steady trail of blood, but thankfully also a lot of footprints to follow. Grandfather hardly needs my young eyes to spot them. His body is transformed from the exhausted, almost defeated man to the strong Elder I remember him as. After ten minutes of following the gruesome track, my mind swirling with the possibilities of what we might uncover, Grandfather stops to look at something I can't see.

'What is it?' I whisper, huddling close, not taking my eyes off the bush ahead of us.

'It's hard to tell. See here? The footprints are smudged and broken,' he replies in a hushed tone.

I hadn't noticed. It looks the same as the others at first glance, but I can see what he is talking about. It is as if someone had stepped on something leaving their print either side and the part in the middle the same texture as the ground. Grandfather points to another interrupted track. The edges are smudged and blurred. Another looks as though half the print had never even been there.

'What do you think it is?' I whisper, my body tensing. I pick up a sharp rock from the ground. I notice Grandfather touch the bag pocket where his knife is carried.

'There is only one thing I know that might leave a track like that,' Grandfather pauses. 'The Lightfoot.'

Shivers shoot down my spine and my hairs stand on end. My body reacting to the name.

Grandfather adds, 'They leave no tracks.'

'What ... what does it want?' Shame as I stumble on my words. I've heard enough rumours and stories.

'They carry out retribution to those who have done terrible things. It's what the other Elders feared for Mr Henry yesterday,' Grandfather explains the old time story. My head spins. It makes sense old Henry getting payback. But why now? Sly grog has ruined enough lives and now people are overdosing on the harder drugs old Henry helped bring into town. The old people won't even look at pictures of dead people. Michael's brother's death still hurts, fresh.

'Do you remember the details of who was hurt by that girl in the hit and run?' Grandfather asks.

I remember the details well; we'd been in town for a funeral. The story had been all over the local news. There had been a candlelight vigil out the front of the hospital where that little girl lay for three nights. She died on the fourth day. There was community outrage when Hannah was let off with a suspended sentence and community work. The young girl's family called it corruption – everyone knew Hannah's city mother had connections to the State Government. It would have helped that her father's side of the family owned one of the largest cattle stations in our area. Our teachers gave us the school's official spiel about the word of the law being the end of it, that bullying wouldn't be tolerated, and that Hannah was just as welcome at our school as everyone else. I'm sure the family's generous donations might have had something to do with how the teachers spoke. I remember feeling amazed that she had the guts to come back to school. And even more so that she didn't seem a bit remorseful.

But who was I to judge? My prank might have just cost Brooklyn and Jenny their lives.

'Yes, Grandfather. She was only four,' I reply. 'An only child. Her parents have moved away now.'

'It might all be connected. The two things that drew the Lightfoot out to rebalance our Law,' he says solemnly. 'At least we know what we might be up against.'

'What will you do if we see it?' I ask, trying to remember back through all the stories told around camp fires when I was young.

'I don't know. I know they are fast. Quiet. Stealth is their biggest strength. And it's not ours,' Grandfather motions towards my injured leg and his.

'I want to get to higher ground,' I say. 'We need to signal again, Grandfather.'

Grandfather considers my request looking towards the sky, searching for the smoke of our previous signal fire. He nods.

'Yes, we can assess what's up ahead as well. Plan to our advantage if we are dealing with a Lightfoot.'

The fact that we are even discussing the possibility of the mythical is crazy. And yet I feel its existence with every bone in my body. Bones I hope to keep in my body.

'This way. I know a songline that leads to a good vantage point at the top of the next rise.'

My legs ache as we climb the steep slope. Rocks tumble and I wonder how far our noise is travelling.

Grandfather stops. We look out over the top of the thick bushland below us. I look back to where I think we have come from. I see a thin line cutting through the bush and rocks, it wouldn't be clear unless you knew it was there.

I search for a clear spot to start a signal fire. Seeing a wide boulder I motion my grandfather over. He nods his approval of the location. I hunt around to find stones to build a wind block and build a small fire.

14
BLOOD

Grandfather sits down and stares out over the valley.

'We need to get back down there. They don't stand a chance against a Lightfoot without us,' Grandfather's voice is edged in fear.

I look at my frail grandfather. I hadn't really noticed how old he had gotten until now. Back in community, doing everyday things he is still a strong role model. He still bosses the rest of us around.

'You wait up here. Hail a chopper if it comes?' I try to convince my grandfather.

Even if it isn't a Creation being that awaits us, even if it is just feral dogs or snakes or spiders, even if it is just massive bleeding injuries ... All we have is a little knife and a small first-aid kit.

'We have ancient blood lines. I have shared with you many of our Creation stories. I have taken you hunting and camping on Country since you were small. I'll be blowed if you are going to dump me too,' Grandfather argues. 'We have something ... even if I haven't remembered what yet.'

I want to tell him of my role in the accident ... that it wasn't an accident, that it was my fault. But I am filled with shame and guilt and can't bring myself to let him down.

We walk down the hill again, Grandfather keeping a fast pace. I lead us back to the blood trail and soon we are moving forward to the unknown.

The sounds of the bush set me on edge.

Out of the corner of my eye I see a flash of white. I turn. The bushes shake and rustle.

'Grandfather, over there,' I whisper. He reaches into his bag for his knife. I slowly bend down and grasp a branch. I feel exposed.

'This way,' Grandfather motions that we should retreat. I follow him, happy to be heading in the opposite direction of whatever's out there. I place one foot carefully behind the other and retreat away from the noise.

There's another rustle, and roosting cockatoos burst from the bushes, flying skywards.

'Just birds.' Grandfather puts the knife safely back. I keep hold of my branch.

'How will we know if something is a Lightfoot?' I ask, sick of feeling so vulnerable and useless against this ancient thing that seems to have the upper hand. Is it hunting? Are we its prey? I want to be prepared.

'They blend in with the bush. They are fast,' Grandfather shares. 'They are human.'

'Human?' I say, amazed. The Lightfoot that Grandfather has me believing in is a human?

'Bushmen. Powerful Law men. Respected in our Culture. More than just you and I,' he adds. 'The only way you can identify them is when they have snuck up on you and you look down at their feet.'

I feel a little relieved ... they're only human. But then again, a respected Law man seeking justice is probably just as scary as a bloodthirsty beast.

'They can't have travelled much further, losing all that blood,' Grandfather whispers, pointing to more splatters.

I know he is right.

15
FOUND

We find the year 12s sitting around quietly and staring, dazed, into a small creek. They are shocked to see us. Their eyes open wide, mouths dropped, frozen mid movement.

'Oh thank goodness,' gasps Brooklyn as she spots us walking through the bush. She goes to raise her right arm in greeting but pulls it down wincing. 'Grandfather!'

My grandfather pulls her in for a gentle hug and pat on the back. My legs feel weak from relief as Brooklyn hobbles over to me.

'Where is everyone else? How are *you* here?' she asks as the rest of the group gather around, tired but excited. I don't even know how to answer. Grandfather moves me gently aside. He holds Brooklyn's face in his hands and brushes the dried blood from her hair.

'They are coming,' he replies gently. 'We just took the lead.'

I look at the dishevelled group. A few of them have strips of old bloodied bandages or ripped clothes wrapped around an arm or a leg. Dixon lies unmoving under the shade of a tree with Miranda watching over him, dabbing a wet cloth on his head.

Jenny is standing between Brooklyn and Ailee. Even after three days out bush she looks amazing. Her hair is pulled back in a loose ponytail, her pants rolled up around her knees showing off her defined legs. She gives me a shy smile. I walk over, suddenly self-conscious. I wonder if she has told her friends about me.

'Are you okay?' I ask. I want to stroke her face, pull her close and tell her everything will be okay like I had that night.

'It's been a pretty crazy few days, Dek,' she replies. 'I'm glad you're here.'

'Dek get over here with that bag.' Grandfather's attention turns to Ms Pritchard. 'Are you okay? Who is hurt?' he asks her, peeling the bag off my back to get the first-aid kit.

'Few injuries, a serious one,' Ms Pritchard says, motioning to Dixon. 'But we aren't all here. Hannah is missing.'

'Let's check him over first and then you can fill us in with the rest about her,' I say, mind swirling with questions about Hannah but knowing we need to check on those that are here first.

Grandfather and I walk over with Ms Pritchard to check on Dixon. His eyes are closed, breathing rapid and uneven, blood seeping through a cloth wrapped around his thigh. Miranda, her eyes streaked with tears, moves aside as Grandfather kneels down beside him.

'He seemed okay when we left the bus,' Miranda begins to sob again.

'I think it might be an infection,' Ms Pritchard wrings her hands anxiously. 'He was okay the first two days; he hasn't woken up properly since this morning.'

Grandfather places the back of his hand on Dixon's brow. And shakes his head.

'I have my first-aid training,' Ms Pritchard says, looking through the first-aid kit, 'but there is only so much we can do here with this.'

My grandfather pulls his body up as if it is suddenly heavy. He looks slowly around the makeshift camp site and walks over to lean against a tree by the edge of the clearing. Ms Pritchard busies herself changing Dixon's injury with cream and a fresh bandage from the kit.

I feel useless. I get the remaining dried food and water that the wild dogs hadn't mauled and count out equal portions, trying to be useful. The year 12s peel off to sit in small groups around the clearing. Brooklyn waves me over to sit with her, Ailee and Jenny on a log by the edge of the clearing.

I feel my cheeks flush red as I walk over and sit down next to my cousin. I sneak another look at Jenny. She is twisting a blade of grass in her fingers, eyes down. The other girls' words tumble out as they rush to beat each other to recall the drama.

'You should have seen your face when the tyre burst and we went over,' Brooklyn teases Ailee as they retell the story.

'It was pretty scary! I've never held onto something so tight. Lucky I didn't break your hand!' Ailee smiles back, exhausted.

'I can't believe we got stranded, bi,' Brooklyn says. 'Proper rookie mistake.'

‘That’s not the worst of it though,’ Ailee gushes. ‘Remember the first night? I was just outside the tree line, doing my business or whatever, I swear I saw a figure. Brook or Jenny have had to come with me every time I take a piss now. Proper buddies now or what?’

Brooklyn laughs. Jenny forces a small smile. I bet it’s the first time she has since the accident. I’m not sure any of us should be laughing just yet. We still need to be rescued. I wonder what’s playing on her mind though. The stuff between us or waiting for rescue.

‘Yeah and then the dead bird that floated down the river when that prissy princess was having a drink!’ Brooklyn added. ‘She wouldn’t drink the creek water from then on.’

I let out a scoff. We all know who she’s talking about.

Dixon lets out a shallow moan as Grandfather lifts his head to squeeze a few drops of water from a strip of cloth into his mouth. ‘We have to keep him hydrated. Small sips as often as we can.’

‘You guys seen any bush medicine around camp?’ I ask, motioning with my lips towards Dixon.

‘I don’t remember that stuff since I was a little one. Kind of feel shame about it now we need it though,’

Brooklyn mutters, flicking her hand in the way us mob do to mean 'nothing'.

'There might be something out that way,' Jenny purses her lips off to the other side of the small creek. 'Want me to show you?'

The tense feeling that had been building in my belly since hearing the news is pushed down by butterflies.

'Yeah, alright,' I agree, jumping up off the log a little too eagerly, sending a sharp pain down my leg.

Leaving Brooklyn and Ailee sitting on the log, Jenny and I walk towards the other side of the clearing and into the thin bush.

'I'm glad you're okay out here,' I say, bending down to check some flowers dangling from a low shrub, avoiding her eyes.

'Yeah, could have been worse,' Jenny shrugs, walking further into the bush.

'Are we okay?' I ask, voice tight, revealing the nerves that I had hoped to hide.

'Yeah, Dek,' Jenny stops to look back at me. 'Just back to normal.'

'What if I don't want to be just "normal" with you again,' I almost want to snatch the words back as they tumble out of my mouth. Before it was just awkwardness. Now I've opened myself up for her to tell me how much of an idiot I've been, laugh in my face or worse.

'You didn't even call me after that night, bi,' Jenny looks down at her shoes. 'Like I was nothing.'

From the corner of my eye I notice what we are looking for. The bush medicine I'd seen my grandmother use when she'd sliced her arm grabbing me from the jaws of a cheeky dog when I was younger. I'd come out of the ordeal almost scratch free. She'd made me search the bush along the road, describing the plant. She had told me how it was meant to stop infection. Lost in the memory I bend down and collect enough to help Dixon. I turn to go back towards the camp.

'You ignoring me again, Dek?' Jenny stares after me, mouth open, eyebrows drawn, a red blush creeping up her cheeks.

'I was shame,' I mutter, plant dangling from my fingers. 'A run amuck bush bloke like me, with someone deadly like you? Thought you'd wake up in the morning and never want to look at me again.'

Jenny reaches out to touch the plant in my fingers, brushing my hand. 'Not too bad for a run amuck bush kid.'

I smile. The louder moans from the camp break the moment.

'We better get this back to him,' Jenny rushes ahead. Nobody stirs as we walk back into the clearing. Everyone is tense again. Some avoid looking towards him, others are huddled around.

'This should help draw out the fever,' I explain to Ms Pritchard as I smear a paste on Dixon's forehead. 'And this should help with the infection.'

Grandfather nods his approval as I rub it in. Taking a deep breath he looks around the rest of the students.

'Okay, now tell us about Hannah,' Grandfather instructs.

'Hannah?' Ms Pritchard replies, voice full of worry. 'She just walked off early morning. I couldn't chase her; my duty of care was to everyone.'

'Why are you even out here?' I ask, a little harsher than I should. My nerves and the stress of the day taking their toll. Ms Pritchard is a newish teacher out here; this trip is probably her first time running a camp out bush. It's just her talk of 'duty of care' was pretty rich given she'd just dumped them all in the middle of nowhere.

Ms Pritchard blushes, 'I was stupid. I intended to drive through to the main campground. But we took a little side track to stop for a bathroom break just off the main road. I saw the old hut and that way in looked good enough, maybe even quicker. So we took that way in. You know, get this rowdy bunch out to set up camp,' Ms Pritchard motions around at all the students now sitting down eating or tending their wounds.

'There must have been some big rains upstream though, cause that river flooded,' Aaron butts in.

'We got through a few small crossings but it had eroded the road away just past the old camp site,' Ms Pritchard continues. 'I thought, we are out bush. You know just go with the flow. There are sites all over this park the kids could use for their assignments. So we backtracked and jumped out at the old camp site. I thought we'd just spend one night here and then head back the way we had come and get back on plan.

'When we arrived at that old campground it felt like we were cursed. It was like every biting bush creature had moved in. Think some tourists had left rubbish in the bush and we were trying to set up with huge ants and feral dogs. Brooklyn remembered Old Macy taking her down a fire access track to go camping and fishing. She said it was close and the perfect clearing and sheltered for a camping spot. It was getting dark by then and we just needed to set up camp. We didn't even get close though before I hit something. Must have been a bird from all the feathers. The tyre burst and I lost control on the dirt corrugation.' Ms Pritchard's voice cracks and tears fill her eyes.

Brooklyn takes over the story. 'It was pretty scary getting out! I thought we were all dead for sure. I busted my arm, few of us had twisted ankles and cuts and some were pretty busted up. We knew we needed to call for help. That bloody sat phone died before we even had a chance to use it. Aaron said we should go up a hill and try his phone he'd snuck in his bag. We thought it might get reception higher up,' she explains. 'But Miss wouldn't let us separate in case we got lost or hurt or whatever. So we took some meat and water, thinking we could set a signal fire and camp on the hill while we waited for help.'

'But all the blood?' I ask.

'Our esky tipped over in the crash; it spilt all the meat we'd packed for the week,' Ms Pritchard remembers. 'Some of us looked a bloody mess when we climbed out of the bus. I thought I'd killed them!' Looking down at Dixon, she says, 'Maybe I have.'

Grandfather asks, 'Why didn't you just go back to the bus?'

'We couldn't. It was such slow going,' she says. 'We couldn't get very far up the hill with these students hurt. But we couldn't get reception anyway. It got dark and we got lost looking for the way back to the bus.'

Brooklyn and Jenny should have known how to find the way back to the bus. Although I felt for them, injured and stressed, trying to keep everyone together. Add in the dark and changing water courses with the flooded creeks from the storm upriver. I assumed it had been a while since that mob had been out this side of the park too. I couldn't blame them. I'd worried about the same thing yesterday.

'Well, let's light you a signal fire now. You mob, start collecting twigs and branches ... but stay within eyesight,' I direct, suddenly eager to get things done. I turn back to Ms Pritchard. 'When did you last see Hannah?'

'She went to the toilet really early. After all the strange things that had been happening, I should have made them all go everywhere in twos. She just never came back.'

'Yeah and she took the last of the bottled water with her to wash her hands!' Rocky complains. 'We are stuck out in the bloody bush, with bloody flooded creeks and she cares about keeping her hands all manicured and dirt free with filtered water! Bloody greedy cow.'

That seems to fit in with what I remember of Hannah. Spoilt and self-absorbed. She didn't fit in with us country mob and she didn't want to. I think she'd happily move to the city if she ever had the chance. I am surprised her parents hadn't sent her to stay there after the accident. Pride I suppose.

'Lucky Jenny was able to show us how to dig soaks to filter the creek water,' Rocky grabs Jenny around the shoulders with a smile. My throat grows tight with jealousy. Three days lost out bush, sleeping together under the stars; that could draw people close. Jenny returns the smile but I don't think it reaches her eyes.

'And the girls were able to get us extra bushtucker and help us set up a base,' Ms Pritchard added. 'We decided it was best to bunker down and wait for help. I couldn't risk leaving in case Hannah came back, and with Dixon getting worse it would have been too hard trying to make our way back with the injured.'

'Do you have any idea which direction your hill was?' Grandfather asks. 'Did it have any special features?'

'A large rock perched on top. Other than that, it was like all these bloody hills out here.' The tension of the past few days was clear on Ms Pritchard's face. 'I think it might be back that direction. We were pretty shocked and disorientated after the crash.'

Grandfather paces the perimeter of the waterhole looking for clues about which way the group had come.

'It's hard to pick up the older trail with all the activity around here now,' he says when he joins us again. 'We'll start in the direction you pointed and see what we can find.'

'How far back are the others?' Ms Pritchard asks, looking back in the direction we had come into the clearing.

'They shouldn't be too far,' replies my grandfather. 'They'd be closing the search area by now.'

I hope he is right. Now the adrenaline and maybe the bush medicine has subsided, the ant bite on my leg has begun to burn again. I wonder if it is infected. Looking at Dixon, it would only be karma if my bite was.

Grandfather nudges my shoulder. 'Let's get moving.'

I am exhausted. I need to speak with Jenny again, explain properly. Plus, with Dixon not doing well and if anything has happened to Hannah, I am still at fault for their injuries ... and I don't want to face a Lightfoot with that on my conscience.

A sense of urgency washes over me. I want this over. I want her found now. I turn and walk into the bush.

16
PAYBACK

The morning sun sends warm rays of light dappling through the thick bush. It is a beautiful time of day to be out here. If it weren't for the burning pain in my leg, the lost girl and possibly a murdering Lightfoot ... it would be a lovely day to be out on Country!

I pick up the track again after a few minutes. With the occasional rubbish the 12s dropped along the way, footprints and trampled grass, the track is easy to follow.

I limp along, Grandfather using a stick to walk behind me. I let my mind wander, eyes and ears still alert for any sign of Hannah ... or anything else.

The sense of relief I had felt about finding Brooklyn, Jenny and the 12s is replaced by a tight chest and knotted belly. As we weave our way along the edge of a now damp riverbed, I stumble on the uneven rocks. As we walk further, Grandfather slips too, dropping his stick. I rush to help him up.

'Grandfather, I'm worried about just leaving the others. Hannah will be easier to spot from the air as soon as that chopper gets here,' I try to convince the old man to turn back. 'We've been hiking for almost two days; you need to rest.'

'Something is drawing me out here,' Grandfather walks up to the shade of a tree and rests against it. 'Can't you feel it?'

I don't really know what I feel any more. The conflict I had felt about leaving my big AFL opportunity to help Grandfather find that mob missing, the pressure to find them before the selection match, the disappointment at missing my big opportunity, relief at finding almost everyone alive, the guilt about the crash and Dixon's injury, the fear for what we might find or who might find us ... I'm exhausted from feeling. The anxiety building in the pit of my stomach is hard to ignore ... and yet he is right, there is something drawing us forward – something we can't control.

I link my arm around his waist and together we hobble on forward. We reach the fallen boulders and large rocks piled at the bottom of the hill within half an hour. Exhausted I look up along the ridge. We'd get a better view from there if she was wandering around the base somewhere ... or if she was hurt up there. We hear the hum of a helicopter in the distance. It gives me the energy we need to begin the climb. I walk carefully behind my grandfather, spotting him in case he slips again.

'The search party won't be far from finding the others,' Grandfather comments at the noise, his tone lighter than I have heard since this all started. 'Let's spread out along this ridge to see if we can pick up Hannah's trail. Stay within eyesight and call if you find anything.'

I don't want to spread out. Grandfather is unsteady and I can't risk him hurt out here. But if it means finding this girl and getting back home quicker, I will do almost anything. It's hard not to feel bitter towards her; it's her selfish actions that are putting us at risk further.

I limp along the rocky outcrop. The rocks are slippery and break apart easily under foot. I inhale sharply. I'm paying such close attention to where my feet are placed that I don't realise I have lost sight of Grandfather.

'Grandfather?' I yell.

'All good, I can hear you!' he replies from behind the slope of the hill. 'Found something?'

'Nothing yet,' I reply.

I feel so guilty. Ultimately, despite Hannah, it was my actions that led us here. I whisper the words to myself that I am too afraid to tell Grandfather: 'It was me. I busted that tyre.'

I wish I was brave enough to tell him. I just can't bear to face his disappointment.

A loud thud behind startles me and I spin around.

Standing about twenty metres away is the ranger. His uniform and dark skin must have helped him blend into the bush as I walked that way.

'You nearly scared me to death!' I exclaim. 'Thank god you found us!'

'We can't have you scared to death,' the ranger replies, speaking thick traditional language and Kriol, voice strong and ominous. 'That's not payback.'

The ranger is walking calmly along the cliff edge towards me. I'm confused by his reply. I step back from the edge a little and look around for the other rescuers. My eye catches on Hannah, lying sprawled down at the bottom of the cliff. She's not moving. No one could survive that fall.

'She slipped and fell,' the ranger says, noticing the direction of my gaze. I get the feeling he is leaving out part of the story.

I'm shocked. I've never seen a dead person before. My brain stops processing everything.

Suddenly the ranger is by my side. He's holding my shoulders securely. He's fast, I think to myself; years of ranger work sure makes you confident on your feet.

'Stop!' yells my grandfather. I turn my head. Stop what?

The ranger's grip tightens on my shoulders, his nails cut into my flesh.

'You don't want him,' Grandfather has a pleading tone in his voice, moving slowly towards us. My heart misses a beat. My eyes drop to the ground. 'He's an innocent one. He's our mob.'

Feathers are at the ranger's feet.

'You're mistaken, brother,' the Lightfoot growls. 'Your sick one back at camp and that one down there are on his head.'

My grandfather looks down the hill and slowly back up to meet my eye.

'It was just a prank. We were just mucking around with scrap metal after school. We never knew a camp was planned. Or that they'd take the bus. Or that it would get this far!' I manage to get the words out to defend myself. 'Why didn't she just stay with her group?'

'Please, this doesn't need punishment; it was an accident,' Grandfather says. He is within a few metres of us now. 'You and I both know the Law.'

'This one's not an innocent,' the Lightfoot replies. My head is spinning. I think my knees might give way. 'There must be payback.'

'There must, you are right,' Grandfather agrees.

'What can you offer in exchange?'

Grandfather holds up his arms, open, offering himself as a sacrifice. 'I am old.'

17
THE EXCHANGE

'You are,' the Lightfoot agrees. 'I have no appetite for payback with you. Your mob back in town need you.'

'How can we make this even?' Grandfather begs. I have never seen my proud and strong grandfather plead with anyone. Now he stands humbled, shoulders slumped ... and all for me.

The Lightfoot withdraws his hunting knife from its sheath at his waist. I hold my breath, waiting for the blade to pierce my skin. He throws me against the hillside, jarring my shoulder and sending shooting pain down my side. He squats down beside me, knife to my throat.

'It is hard keeping the Law with so many of our mob caught up in wrong these days,' the Lightfoot says, sounding more human than beast. My grandfather mirrors the other man by squatting down where he is, listening, watching the blade move with the pulse on my neck. 'So many following white man's law, they have forgotten our Law.'

Grandfather nods in agreement. 'I hear you, brother,' he responds. 'Is there any chance my grandson can do payback another way?'

'It is hard to be everywhere at once. I am old. Times have changed,' the Lightfoot continues. 'He will stay with me. He will pay back his blood debt with service.'

'No,' I yell, reaching for my grandfather. The Lightfoot's knife digs into my flesh. It hurts, but not more than the desperate knot in my stomach.

'You know there is no other way.' The Lightfoot ignores my cries and stares at my grandfather.

Grandfather looks down towards the dead girl. He nods.

The Lightfoot drags me to my feet. I want to struggle, but the knife is sharp, and the drop is steep. I flop like a dead weight in the Lightfoot's arms. I want to scream out, escape, run to the rescue party getting ever closer in their search. But I saw how fast the Lightfoot can move. I will never outrun him with my injured leg. Plus, I can't just leave my grandfather behind with him.

The Lightfoot pushes me forward along the edge of the hill, knife digging in under my ribs. I look back over my shoulder. My grandfather holds his body up with one hand, head cradled into the other, sobbing.

18
DISTANCE

I'm distracted from the growing pain in my leg by the sharp sting of the blade against my skin. The Lightfoot keeps us walking over the hard, rocky ground and has avoided the softer earth near the cover of trees. Sweat drips down my forehead and back. I am too scared to even swipe the flies away from my face in case the knife finds its mark.

I am relieved to hear the hum of a rescue helicopter build up again in the distance. I assume that means they have found and loaded on some of the year 12s. I wonder if my grandfather has made it back and reported my abduction yet. I wonder if they will get straight on our trail or finish the rescue before searching for me.

I can hear the breathing of the Lightfoot behind me as he pushes me forward, unhappy with my pace. The push sends shooting pain up from my leg through my body.

My anger boils, 'So did you kill Hannah? Payback for the hit and run?'

As soon as the words have left my lips my heart skips with fear. The thought I had been holding back since seeing her dead body had slipped from my mouth without me even thinking. Does the guilt lay with me or did he kill her? Did he kill old Henry too? Did he play a part in all the drama these last few days?

The Lightfoot doesn't answer. He also doesn't stab me or punish me for talking. I have to be thankful for the small things I suppose ... like still being alive.

The Lightfoot pushes me forward again. I can feel his frustration at my slow pace. I'm exhausted. With a grunt and surprising strength, he lifts me over his shoulder. I'm not light, toned for my age from playing so much sport. This is big shame; I'm not a little kid who can be carried around! I consider the option of pulling his hair or biting into his back that is pressed against my face. I realise quickly that would just anger him.

We don't have far to go; I am relieved when his footfalls slow.

'Stay,' he commands, flipping me off his shoulder and pointing to a log. I hobble over and sit. I watch him as he prepares some berries and leaves. He hands me the mush and points to the red, raised bump on my leg. I obey, rubbing the ointment in. I take my time, slowly. Hoping that the more time I waste here the more time the search party will have to find me.

'Up.' Tired of waiting, he drags me to my feet.

My leg still hurts but I can walk. I wonder if the bush medicine has made a difference to Dixon or if he has been airlifted to hospital yet. I don't have to walk long before we reach the bottom of a rocky outcrop. He points me under the shade of the rocks.

'Rest,' he commands. I lay my head against the ground keeping my eye on the Lightfoot as he dusts my footprints away.

19
SHOCK

I don't know how I could have fallen asleep on the hard, uneven earth. But I did.

The night is dark and humid. A shiver runs down my spine. It is quiet in the bush now. No more vehicle noise. Just the noises of the bush. My legs ache ... but the bite no longer hurts. My heart aches too. All I want is to be safely at home with my family. Mum cooking dinner of stew on the stove, me fighting my cousins for whose turn it is to choose the TV channel, Grandfather stoking the fire.

The Lightfoot has withdrawn his knife from my back. He knows I have nowhere to run. I tossed up all my options of escape on the long walk. Somehow knocking him over when we walk over the uneven rocky surfaces of a hill, a large rock on the head while he rests, tackling him for the knife. He is old, but his muscles ripple under taut skin, and if he has superhuman speed along ancient songlines ... Injured and exhausted, I don't stand a chance. He sits on a rock a few metres away from me looking at the swaying trees. Alert. The soft moonlight has slightly lit up the area in front of us but the rest is blurred in darkness. I have no idea where we are.

The Lightfoot notices that I am awake. He moves his head indicating that I should get up. I push my body up into sitting position and pull myself up.

'I'm just slowing you down. They'll be here with a chopper soon. You should probably just leave me,' my voice is weak as I try to convince the old man to let me go. 'I didn't kill that girl.'

The Lightfoot pushes me on in silence. I wonder what Jenny did when Grandfather returned without me? Or what my mum said when Grandfather returned? I wonder what my mates will think? What will the police do? Surely they will send a search party out again? Or will resources be spread too thin between old Henry, the car crash, rescuing that mob, rushing Dixon to hospital, Hannah and now me?

Surely, we can't have travelled too far from where they found everyone and that will make their search easier? Had it all been random or connected? How did the Lightfoot tie into it all?

I had expected that we would return to his little hut by now but we haven't. I am exhausted, physically and mentally. My tummy rumbles, forcing me to be brave enough to ask, 'When will we get to the tourist shed? I am starving.'

The Lightfoot laughs. 'We aren't going to that place.'

I am shocked. Despair washes over me.

'But ...' I begin.

'That was never my place,' he said slowly. If it wasn't his hut ... where is the ranger?

'The ranger slipped and fell too,' the Lightfoot says as if sensing my next question, his soft voice somehow menacing. 'It's dangerous work hunting animals. Especially those protected by white man's conservation laws and our Dreaming.'

Deeper into the bush we walk. So much has happened that my head spins. I struggle to focus. This new information changes everything. Did the Lightfoot plan the whole thing from the very start. Did it start with the ranger or old Henry? Is he responsible for all the drama that has happened the last few days? A whirlwind of retribution.

'And old Henry?' I can barely force the words from my lips. 'The crash?'

The Lightfoot grunts, 'There are a lot of people who do not follow the old ways.'

The Lightfoot stops by a river and listens. I have no choice but to stand silently too, waiting to see his next move.

'Listen,' he instructs. 'Pay close attention to the sounds.'

I do, because the starlight is so dim it is hard to see much detail to rely on sight alone.

'Hear that sound?' the Lightfoot says as birds chatter, readjusting themselves in the trees. He throws his knife in that direction. His years of experience obvious as he confidently walks into the dark, returning with a bird on the end of his knife.

'Collect some wood,' I am told next. I stumble around the riverside, collecting dried branches while listening to the frogs and the dull thud of the knife striking. I wish I could just run while he is busy but he'd find me.

I set my bundle of sticks at the Lightfoot's feet. He moves them to a rock by the water and sets a small pile of dried grass underneath. He pulls a flint from his pocket and strikes with precision. A spark flies and he blows steadily. A small fire begins to burn. I wonder if there is a search party looking for me. What has Grandfather told them? Will they see this fire in the dark night?

We eat the collection of small animals in silence. My tummy is grateful for the food. Tiredness forces me to speak to my captor again.

'How long till we sleep?'

'We are nearly there,' the Lightfoot replies. When we finish eating, he throws dirt on our fire and then kicks the half-burnt sticks into the river. He scoops up water and washes the rock clean.

'Take off your shoes,' he commands. 'Put them in your pack.'

I imagine all the snakes and spiders just waiting to bite me in the undergrowth. But I obey; it might be better to die of a snakebite than live the rest of my life with this man.

He leads us through the shallow river for a few hundred metres. We step out onto a small pebble bank. My feet tingle with the cold.

'Put your shoes back on,' he commands again. I feel like a puppet. Frustrated at his change of mind ...

I realise he is trying to hide our scent from tracking dogs. The Lightfoot stands nearby waiting. I stay knelt down and try to scratch a cross in the rock with the edge of my nails. The Lightfoot doesn't notice. I wonder if he would even care if he did, my tiny mark in the vast wilderness. My tiny glimmer of hope.

I stand up shivering. Waiting for his next command.

'Tonight, you will begin to learn the sounds of the bush. You will learn your Country,' he says. I don't want to learn anything. I want to curl up on the hard rocks and fall asleep right here. Then it occurs to me; if I listen and learn I might soon be able to move like him ... then I can escape.

It feels like hours before we reach a small cave at the bottom of a hill. I can't sleep. He snores. This mythical Lightfoot, feared by man, woman and child, is snoring.

20

WATCH AND LEARN

As the days go by, the Lightfoot watches me less intensely. The knife is sheathed more often. I have more freedom. We are deep in the wilderness now.

The Lightfoot is quiet most of the time, uttering commands or short explanations of bush food, how to track an animal, how to build our shelters, mostly stuff I already know. At night though, he shares Creation stories. It reminds me of my grandfather. I miss home.

The first few days I had hope that around the next hill my grandfather would be standing with a brigade of police. The next few weeks I hoped that the Lightfoot would realise his mistake at choosing such a terrible apprentice and just let me go. After that I wondered about my chances of the Lightfoot just having a heart attack from old age.

The long quiet hours give me lots of time to think. After hours of regret about my tyre prank, and the crash, and Dixon and Hannah, about my missed football opportunity, I almost wish the Lightfoot had pushed me off the cliff. My thoughts turn to Jenny. How does she feel about my disappearance? Is she angry that we didn't have a chance to talk properly before I left? Has Rocky been there to comfort her ... or more?

It hurts. I can't waste days wishing for things I can't control. I push the thoughts from my mind, focusing on the rhythm of the wind, the sounds of the bush.

One day, close to the new year by my guess, the Lightfoot announces, 'It's time you went through Law.'

My heart skips with joy. Culture time? That might be with other Elders! My chance to go home might be right around the corner. Or will the other Elders be in awe of the Lightfoot and just accept that I am now his apprentice? Could a countryman there pass on a message to my grandfather?

We set off early. I remember back just a few weeks ago, maybe a few months ago now, when I had struggled to drag myself out of bed for school. Here, we wake up before the sun every morning, just as the first animals stir. I don't mind any more; I am almost excited about what I learn each new day.

The hike is long. Sometimes, I feel sure we'll come across a community out here. Sometimes, I am so absorbed watching the land, listening to sounds, that I forget to care about being rescued.

'Stop, we must wait here,' the Lightfoot announces when we have crossed a shallow river. 'Fetch the wood for a fire.'

I obey instantly, returning with kindling and a large log.

'We'll need more than that. Our fire tonight is a signal to that other mob that we are here,' the Lightfoot flicks his head in the direction in front of us.

It is early the next morning when they come for us. I don't hear or sense them as I sit bleary-eyed by the camp fire. I sit up, startled; Lightfoot puts a hand on my leg to steady me. I watch as a small group of Elders slowly walk in silence to join us around the fire. It is not my place to speak.

21
LAW

The days here are more intense now.

In language I learn the stories of the land, the Law.

I begin to see the fragile connections.

Slowly, I learn about my responsibility.

My honour.

Power.

22

LIGHTFOOT

I move quickly through the hospital corridor, unnoticed.

'Can you believe he's in here again? After the bloody miracle of surviving that crash off the cliff,' an old nurse leans against the reception desk, gossiping.

'Wish it was just him this time. Wish he'd finished himself off. Waste of space,' agrees another, younger nurse sitting in front of the computer.

'I can't believe he was let off so lightly the last time,' the first nurse says, adding details while flicking through a file. 'That poor family.'

'Makes me sick that we have to care for someone like that,' the young nurse says in disgust. 'Bloody drunk.'

'Worst bit is, he gets to lie pain free in that induced coma,' the older woman replies, 'while those boys lie cold in the morgue.'

'A bloody miracle he didn't wipe out the whole bus load of them,' she nods her head towards the ward to her left. I follow their gaze. A boy, about my age, lies on a bed, his football boots set by the wall and his jersey dumped over the guest chair. His footy dreams are over. It occurs to me that my dreams are not. I can walk in both worlds now. Maybe I can still wear those boots one day.

'If the doctors can reduce the swelling on his brain and get him off that respirator, he could make a full recovery,' her face says it all.

I keep my head down and breeze past.

'They should have jailed him for drug driving the last time. Funny how the world works though, that old Henry died the day before the crash that he helped cause. Can't believe the dodgy bastard was getting drugs into towns,' the older nurse taps her files on the desk and turns back to her work. Wordlessly, I find the room and open the door.

He lies alone on the bed.

The Dream Killer.

The Destroyer of Families.

A single vase of flowers sits on the bench next to him. I recognise his wife slumped asleep in the chair. I can still picture her accusing face that day she ran towards me in the back of the troopy.

Tears streak her face.

I wonder if she is crying for her husband or the boys he has killed.

It doesn't matter either way – there will be more tears to come.

My eyes
follow the cords
trailing from his arms
to the beeping machine.

I turn down the volume.

I take a breath.

The thin green line

flatlines ...

Payback.

I am Lightfoot.

GLOSSARY

BRA – brother, mate
DREAMING AND CREATION – the religious, spiritual and fundamental belief system(s) of a First Nations people, that is particular to them
FEED – food
GIVE HIM A HIDING – fight, punishment or beating
HIGH-CLASS – this could mean a few things depending on the context. It generally means stuck up, snobby, rich, well off, or 'acting white' as a put-down
LAW – traditional Aboriginal Law
ROO – kangaroo
SLY GROG – black market alcohol. There are liquor restrictions in many parts of the Northern Territory and Western Australia, especially in Aboriginal towns and communities, which has led to an underground alcohol trade
SONGLINES – significant songs passed down from generation to generation
TOP AREA – the top part of town
TOWNIE – someone who lives in town
TROOPY – Toyota Troop Carrier, commonly used four-wheel drive in remote communities
US MOB – Aboriginal people

CARL MERRISON is a Jaru/Kija man from the Kimberley with a passion for youth issues and voice. He is a youth mentor, football coach and program co-ordinator. Carl was runner-up for the 2016 WA Local Hero Award.

HAKEA HUSTLER is an experienced English teacher who has taught around Australia, including in remote Aboriginal communities. Hakea is committed to Indigenous education with a particular focus on story as learning and empowerment.

Carl and Hakea's debut novella, *Black Cockatoo,* was published by Magabala Books in 2018 and was shortlisted for the Readings Children's Book of the Year, shortlisted in the Children's Book Council of Australia Young Reader category, shortlisted for an Australian Book Industry Award, selected as a feature text for the 2018 Summer Reading Challenge and included in the New South Wales Premier's Reading Challenge 2019.